Better Together

A GUIDE FOR DISCIPLESHIP

THE DAILY GRACE CO.

How to use this resource

Our hope and prayer for this resource is that it would be used as a tool to help establish and guide a discipleship relationship between two individuals or in the context of a small group. Initiating this relationship could be something as simple as approaching someone at church, taking someone out for coffee, bringing it up in conversation, or calling the person up with an invitation to walk through this resource with you. If you do not already have someone in mind, begin praying and thinking through someone you would like to join you.

This resource will guide you through the discipleship relationship and provide material for you to walk through together as you pursue spiritual maturity. The content covered includes sections on how to articulate a testimony, how to share the gospel, how to study the Bible, how to memorize Scripture, and how to cultivate a life of prayer. The intention would be to move through each week together as quickly or as slowly as you would like, focusing on developing those particular disciplines in your life. We hope that your relationship would not end with this resource but would serve as a means of establishing a committed discipleship relationship you are able to continue long after you finish. The goal of discipleship is ultimately that Christians would utilize these types of relationships to flourish in the faith, love God more, and in turn, seek to glorify Him with their lives. We pray that this resource would be a valuable tool in that pursuit.

The inductive method provides tools for deeper and more intentional Bible study. To study a book of the Bible inductively, work through the steps below after reading background information on the book.

1 OBSERVATION & COMPREHENSION
Key question: What does the text say?

After reading the book of the Bible in its entirety at least once, begin working with smaller portions of the book. Read a passage of Scripture repetitively, and then mark the following items in the text:

- Key or repeated words and ideas
- Key themes
- Transition words *(Ex: therefore, but, because, if/then, likewise, etc.)*
- Lists
- Comparisons & Contrasts
- Commands
- Unfamiliar words (look these up in a dictionary)
- Questions you have about the text

2 INTERPRETATION
Key question: What does the text mean?

Once you have annotated the text, work through the following steps to help you interpret its meaning:

- Read the passage in other versions for a better understanding of the text.
- Read cross-references to help interpret Scripture with Scripture.
- Paraphrase or summarize the passage to check for understanding.
- Identify how the text reflects the metanarrative of Scripture, which is the story of creation, fall, redemption, and restoration.
- Read trustworthy commentaries if you need further insight into the meaning of the passage.

3   APPLICATION
Key Question: How should the truth of this passage change me?

Bible study is not merely an intellectual pursuit. The truths about God, ourselves, and the gospel that we discover in Scripture should produce transformation in our hearts and lives. Answer the following questions as you consider what you have learned in your study:

- What attributes of God's character are revealed in the passage?

    Consider places where the text directly states the character of God, as well as how His character is revealed through His words and actions.

- What do I learn about myself in light of who God is?

    Consider how you fall short of God's character, how the text reveals your sin nature, and what it says about your new identity in Christ.

- How should this truth change me?

    A passage of Scripture may contain direct commands telling us what to do or warnings about sins to avoid in order to help us grow in holiness. Other times our application flows out of seeing ourselves in light of God's character. As we pray and reflect on how God is calling us to change in light of His Word, we should be asking questions like, "How should I pray for God to change my heart?" and "What practical steps can I take toward cultivating habits of holiness?"

ATTRIBUTES OF GOD

ETERNAL

God has no beginning and no end. He always was, always is, and always will be.

HAB. 1:12 / REV. 1:8 / IS. 41:4

FAITHFUL

God is incapable of anything but fidelity. He is loyally devoted to His plan and purpose.

2 TIM. 2:13 / DEUT. 7:9
HEB. 10:23

GLORIOUS

God is ultimately beautiful, deserving of all praise and honor.

REV. 19:1 / PS. 104:1
EX. 40:34-35

GOOD

God is pure; there is no defilement in Him. He is unable to sin, and all He does is good.

GEN. 1:31 / PS. 34:8 / PS. 107:1

GRACIOUS

God is kind, giving to us gifts and benefits which we do not deserve.

2 KINGS 13:23 / PS. 145:8
IS. 30:18

HOLY

God is undefiled and unable to be in the presence of defilement. He is sacred and set-apart.

REV. 4:8 / LEV. 19:2 / HAB. 1:13

IMMUTABLE

God does not change. He is the same yesterday, today, and tomorrow.

1 SAM. 15:29 / ROM. 11:29
JAMES 1:17

JEALOUS

God is desirous of receiving the praise and affection He rightly deserves.

EX. 20:5 / DEUT. 4:23-24
JOSH. 24:19

JUST

God governs in perfect justice. He acts in accordance with justice. In Him there is no wrongdoing or dishonesty.

IS. 61:8 / DEUT. 32:4 / PS. 146:7-9

LOVE

God is eternally, enduringly, steadfastly loving and affectionate. He does not forsake or betray His covenant love.

JN. 3:16 / EPH. 2:4-5 / 1 JN. 4:16

MERCIFUL

God is compassionate, withholding us from the wrath that we deserve.

TITUS 3:5 / PS. 25:10
LAM. 3:22-23

OMNIPOTENT

God is all-powerful; His strength is unlimited.

MAT. 19:26 / JOB 42:1-2
JER. 32:27

OMNIPRESENT

God is everywhere; His presence is near and permeating.

PROV. 15:3 / PS. 139:7-10
JER. 23:23-24

OMNISCIENT

God is all-knowing; there is nothing unknown to Him.

PS. 147:4 / I JN. 3:20
HEB. 4:13

PATIENT

God is long-suffering and enduring. He gives ample opportunity for people to turn toward Him.

ROM. 2:4 / 2 PET. 3:9 / PS. 86:15

RIGHTEOUS

God is blameless and upright. There is no wrong found in Him.

PS. 119:137 / JER. 12:1
REV. 15:3

SOVEREIGN

God governs over all things; He is in complete control.

COL. 1:17 / PS. 24:1-2
1 CHRON. 29:11-12

TRUE

God is our measurement of what is fact. By Him are we able to discern true and false.

JN. 3:33 / ROM. 1:25 / JN. 14:6

WISE

God is infinitely knowledgeable and is judicious with His knowledge.

IS. 46:9-10 / IS. 55:9 / PROV. 3:19

Creation

In the beginning, God created the universe. He made the world and everything in it. He created humans in His own image to be His representatives on the earth.

Fall

The first humans, Adam and Eve, disobeyed God by eating from the fruit of the Tree of Knowledge of Good and Evil. Because of sin, the world was cursed. The punishment for sin is death, and because of Adam's original sin, all humans are sinful and condemned to death.

Redemption

God sent his Son to become a human and redeem His people. Jesus Christ lived a sinless life but died on the cross to pay the penalty for sin. He resurrected from the dead and ascended into heaven. All who put their faith in Jesus are saved from death and freely receive the gift of eternal life.

Restoration

One day, Jesus Christ will return again and restore all that sin destroyed. He will usher in a new heaven and new earth where all who trust in Him will live eternally with glorified bodies in the presence of God.

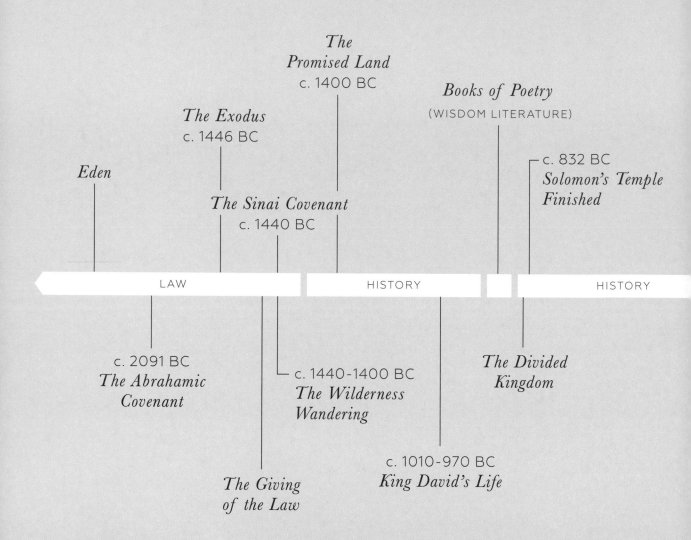

The
Promised Land
c. 1400 BC

Books of Poetry
(WISDOM LITERATURE)

The Exodus
c. 1446 BC

c. 832 BC
Solomon's Temple
Finished

Eden

The Sinai Covenant
c. 1440 BC

LAW

HISTORY

HISTORY

c. 2091 BC
The Abrahamic
Covenant

c. 1440-1400 BC
The Wilderness
Wandering

The Divided
Kingdom

c. 1010-970 BC
King David's Life

The Giving
of the Law

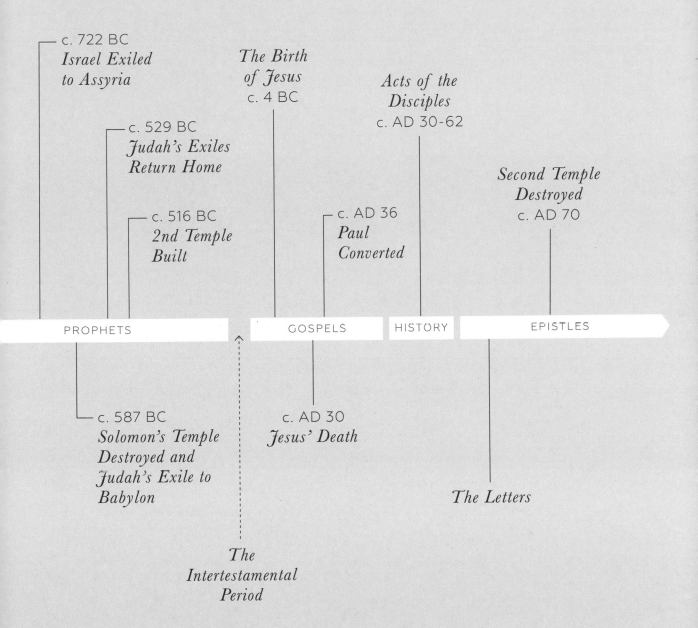

c. 722 BC
*Israel Exiled
to Assyria*

*The Birth
of Jesus*
c. 4 BC

*Acts of the
Disciples*
c. AD 30-62

c. 529 BC
*Judah's Exiles
Return Home*

*Second Temple
Destroyed*
c. AD 70

c. 516 BC
*2nd Temple
Built*

c. AD 36
*Paul
Converted*

PROPHETS

GOSPELS

HISTORY

EPISTLES

c. 587 BC
*Solomon's Temple
Destroyed and
Judah's Exile to
Babylon*

c. AD 30
Jesus' Death

The Letters

*The
Intertestamental
Period*

Before you begin

Part 1: Introduction to Discipleship

Part 2: The Gospel

Table of Contents

Accountability Questions

Accountability is a necessary aspect of discipleship. Christian accountability is essentially giving an account of our lives to one another. It is the realization that we must answer and give an account to God for our actions in life (Romans 2:15-16, 2 Corinthians 5:10), and we are best equipped to pursue godliness when we humbly and vulnerably invite others into our lives to help us along the way (Galatians 6:1-2, Hebrews 10:23-24). Reference a few of the following questions with your discipleship partner each time you meet together. Use this as an opportunity to give an honest assessment of your walk with God—areas of your life where you struggle the most and also where you are most encouraged. Remember this exercise is only helpful if you commit to being honest and vulnerable with one another.

How would you characterize your commitment to Bible study and prayer?

What is God teaching you through the study of His Word?

How has your prayer life been shaping you?

Is there sin you need to confess?

Is there forgiveness you need to seek out?

How have you seen God's sanctifying work in your life?

What spiritual conversations have you had this week?

Are you stewarding your time and resources well?

How have you been honoring and loving those closest to you?

Have you been faithful in the ministry entrusted to you?

Date: / / *Prayer Request:* _____

_____

_____

_____

Date: / / *Prayer Answered:* _____

_____

_____

_____

Date: / / *Prayer Request:* _____

_____

_____

_____

Date: / / *Prayer Answered:* _____

_____

_____

_____

Date: / / *Prayer Request:* _____

_____

_____

_____

Date: / / *Prayer Answered:* _____

_____

_____

_____

Date: / / *Prayer Request:* _____

_____

_____

_____

Date: / / *Prayer Answered:* _____

_____

_____

PART ONE

Introduction to Discipleship

"
We become blood-bought
brothers and sisters, united
under the saving work
of *Jesus Christ.*

"

What is Discipleship?

The beauty of coming to understand the gospel of Jesus Christ is not only that we are invited into a relationship with God but also that we are invited into a relationship with the people of God. We become blood-bought brothers and sisters, united under the saving work of Jesus Christ. As a result, we do not have to do the Christian life alone. We can walk alongside one another, encouraging and exhorting one another, sharing our lives with one another, and helping one another along toward heaven.

Though there are many types of relationships we will find with other Christians, one type of relationship that many of us desire, seek out, or want to understand more about is a discipleship relationship. You may be familiar with this term, or you may be hearing it for the first time. Essentially, a discipleship relationship is one in which an older Christian spends intentional time with a younger Christian, mentoring in the ways of the Christian life, incorporating Scripture, prayer, ministry, fellowship, and the pursuit of holiness. One is able to learn and grow alongside another, observing and asking questions while working out what it means to live as a disciple of Christ and mature in the faith. Using the terms "older" and "younger" does not necessarily pertain to age but rather, experience and wisdom in the faith. These relationships can be one-on-one or in the context of a group. The freedom in discipleship is that it can be flexible and take many shapes and forms. Discipleship relationships can differ depending on the season of life, availability, and expectations. The hope and goal of discipleship is ultimately that Christians would utilize these types of relationships to flourish in the faith, to love God more, and in turn, seek to glorify Him with their lives.

Understanding discipleship is vital to how we implement discipleship. The greatest place for us to consider discipleship is embedded in the life and ministry of Jesus as noted in the Bible. The first time we are introduced to the word "disciple" is in the New Testament in the gospel of Matthew. This term is used generally to describe one who is a follower of a particular person or doctrine. More specifically for Christians, to be a disciple of Jesus Christ is to follow Him and His commands. It is to emulate the life He lived on earth and to share in His purpose and mission.

Jesus called twelve men to be His first disciples, though many others followed Him closely. His requirement was this: "If anyone wants to follow after me, let him deny himself, take up his cross, and follow me" (Matthew 16:24). There is a laying down of one's life that happens in the work of being a disciple. We lay down our lives by letting go of anything that prohibits us from being faithful to the ministry of Jesus—worldly comforts, passions, pleasures, and self-seeking desires. We take up our cross by committing to the work of Jesus even when it is hard, uncomfortable, or costly. This is clear in the continuation of Jesus' discipling ministry. The disciples' primary goal and mission in life was to make Jesus known with their words and actions. Their lives became entrenched in knowing God more so that they might be shaped into Christ's likeness and in turn help others know Him more. This was an active work in the lives of these disciples. It required devoting themselves to the teaching of God's Word, prayer, evangelism, and fellowship so that they might accurately and faithfully emulate the life of Christ to others.

Every Christian is a disciple of Christ, and at the end of Jesus' life, He charged His disciples to go and make more disciples in what is referred to as the Great Commission. Matthew 28:18-20 says, "Jesus came near and said to them, 'All authority has been given to me in heaven and on earth. Go, therefore, and make disciples of all nations, baptizing them in the name of the Father and of the Son and of the Holy Spirit, teaching them to observe everything I have commanded you. And remember, I am with you always, to the end of the age.'" We participate in the work of the Great Commission through both evangelism and discipleship. There is a difference between the two, yet both are necessary. We evangelize by sharing the good news of the gospel with those who have not come to know Jesus as their Lord and Savior. We disciple those who have committed their lives to Christ and follow Him. Discipleship builds upon the fruitful work of evangelism by encouraging long-term growth and faithfulness in everyday life.

As Christians, when we come to salvation, we do not immediately and fully understand how to live and walk faithfully as God intends for us to in this world. It is a lifelong pursuit. With the help of those who have walked faithfully before us, we can grow in our knowledge and understanding of what that looks like. As we grow in our faith, we are able to share the gospel with others and continue the work of discipleship with those who have the same questions we initially did. The continued process of discipleship through generations and generations has allowed each of us to hear and share in the gospel today. Discipleship has served as an instrument in the continuation of the gospel and the faithful service of Christians. There is grace-filled, God-gifted work that is established and continued in and through discipleship relationships. It is an essential and necessary part of the Christian life, and over the next few weeks, we will explore various elements of discipleship and how you can incorporate and practice them in your discipleship relationships.

Write out your personal understanding of discipleship.

_____

_____

_____

Read John 8:31, John 13:34-35, and John 15:8. What characterizes a true disciple of Christ according to these passages?

_____

_____

_____

_____

The purpose of discipleship is to learn to live as a disciple of Christ and to mature in the faith alongside another. Read Ephesians 4:11-16, Hebrews 5:12-14, Philippians 3:7-16. How do these passages characterize one who is mature in the faith?

_____

_____

_____

_____

Share with your discipleship partner specific ways you hope to grow and mature in the faith.

Take time to pray, asking God to equip and shape you specifically in those areas and through your discipleship relationships.

> *Commitment to Scripture*
> is essential to knowing God
> more and growing into the
> likeness of Christ.

Expectations for Discipleship

Discipleship relationships can take many shapes and forms. The beauty of relationships in general is that they do not all look the same. There is a level of freedom in the way we construct and establish them. It is, therefore, necessary to communicate clearly what expectations for the relationship should look like. This process does not have to be an intense conversation but more so a thoughtful consideration of how we hope to invest in this relationship and our time together. As you have hopefully found someone to walk through this study with, it is important to discuss what your time together will look like. By having a conversation about pursuing a discipleship relationship, you can avoid the gray area and confusion of unmet expectations within the relationship. Likewise, a discipleship relationship does not have to be limited to one person. There is beauty in differentiation when learning and growing alongside multiple men or women, as long as we are remaining faithful to our commitments and investing fully in each relationship.

One of the most important elements of a discipleship relationship is a mutual, unbending commitment to God's Word. Commitment to Scripture is essential to knowing God more and growing into the likeness of Christ. There are many differences we will discover in relationships with other Christians. We all have different gifts, experiences, upbringings, and perspectives, but we find an anchor for growing together in our salvation in Christ, and we are united in His mission and purpose through God's Word. This commonality holds insurmountable value in the heart of our discipling relationships.

We must continually hold one another to the standards of Scripture, being quick to elevate it over our own assumptions and feelings. As we seek to discuss and study it together, let us help one another toward lives and hearts shaped and transformed by the truth of Scripture.

Another important element of discipleship relationships is to establish the level of commitment we can make to one another. Some women may be able to spend an hour each week together at a coffee shop. Young moms may need to meet in their home during nap time every other week. Working women may need to squeeze in time before dinner or early Saturday mornings with flexibility. It may even be that multiple women are being discipled by an older woman, meeting together in the form of a small group with a changing schedule to fit everyone's needs. The level of commitment we give to one another should take into consideration our season of life and the amount of time we can realistically invest in the relationship. Be honest and open with one another. When we have this conversation beforehand, we can enter into our time together with proper expectations and a willingness to make the most of our time.

To develop a healthy discipleship relationship it is imperative to remember that discipleship is a partnership in the work of the gospel. There are always ways to learn and grow as both the older and the younger Christian. Therefore, humility and vulnerability are vital in the work of discipleship. We must humble ourselves to the teaching, encouragement, and exhortation of one another in order that we might truly pursue growth. We must remain open and honest about our personal struggles so that we can actively pray for one another. We must remain willing to confess and repent our sin to one another in order to hold one another accountable to the pursuit of holiness. If we hold fast to our pride and shallow confessions, we miss the fruitful work of discipleship, and we rob each other of the opportunity to witness God's changing and sanctifying grace in each other's lives.

Lastly, as we consider expectations for discipleship, our hope is that these relationships would encourage us toward lasting obedience and steadfastness in the faith. Our aim is not only to connect during our scheduled times together but to invest deeply in the lives of one another which requires both truth and grace. We must be willing to enter into one another's struggles to speak the truth when life is hard, and God's Word seems to fall flat on our ears. We must choose to be gracious and compassionate when expectations change, and our relationships take a new shape. Discipleship is not always easy. It can seem like hard work at times, but the fruit of our commitment is more than worth it, and the growth that takes place is preparing us for heaven.

Read Titus 2:1-7. What does it look like to live a life committed to God's Word and sound teaching? Make a list of the characteristics for both older and younger Christians.

_____

_____

_____

_____

_____

Read 2 Timothy 4:3-4 and 1 Timothy 6:3-5. This is what it looks like to live in such a way that rejects commitment to God's Word. Make a list of each characteristic.

_____

_____

_____

_____

_____

How will you hold one another accountable to sound teaching and partnership in the gospel in this relationship?

_____

_____

_____

_____

_____

Take some time to discuss expectations for your discipleship relationship. Think through defining your discipleship relationship, naming your level of commitment, and scheduling a time.

The *call to make disciples*
of all nations is for
every disciple of Christ.

22

Hope for Discipleship

Discipleship is a non-negotiable for Christians. Discipleship is not just for seminary graduates, church leaders, and Bible scholars. The call to make disciples of all nations is for every disciple of Christ. When it comes to the Great Commission, every believer is appointed. There are no spectators in God's global mission. When we are in Christ, we are spiritually alive, and we are called to partner with the Spirit in reproducing this new life in others. We fulfill this call by speaking the truth of the gospel and adorning the gospel with our lives, and we do this together with fellow believers.

In His infinite wisdom, God chooses to use ordinary people to do His work. Discipleship is God's plan of multiplication, but discipleship can be reduced to a simple formula. It is the example that Jesus set forth for us in the New Testament—He called His disciples to Himself and taught them what it meant to follow Him. Likewise, we are to help people understand what it means to follow Jesus as He draws them to Himself. That is the heart of discipleship. Discipleship relationships do not look identical. In fact, they occur in diverse contexts. However, the end goal is the same: to see the glory of God exalted among every people group.

Believers today are called to assume the responsibility of discipleship in our lives. We are to seek the spiritual good of those around us by pointing them to Christ and encouraging them as they grow in Christ-likeness. Joining God in this particular work is an overflow of our own personal discipleship; a natural outworking of following Christ is helping others follow Christ. Our love and devotion to God are expressed in love and care for our neighbors (1 John 4:19-21). This is because engaging in discipleship is obedience to God's command (Matthew 28:19-20), and love and obedience go hand in hand (John 14:15). Discipling is a profound way of loving others as well. Not only are we seeking their eternal wellbeing, but we are equipping them to live out their God-given purpose of knowing, enjoying, and glorifying God.

Discipleship is important, and it is fundamental to the Christian life. As followers of Christ, we are "servants of Christ and managers of the mysteries of God" (1 Corinthians 4:1). We are message bearers of the good news of Jesus Christ. Yet, we also have different abilities and opportunities. We have different spheres of influence. We are members of different local bodies of Christ. While we are each called to be discipled and to disciple others, it can look different from person to person. The message is the same, the end goal is the same, but the details of each of our personal engagements vary. There are many ways we can live out an others-oriented life for the glory of God.

TAKE SOME TIME TO ASSESS YOUR OWN LIFE.

What are unique gifts, talents, or resources that have been entrusted to you?

Who is in your current sphere of influence?

How can you serve in the context of your local church?

The call to make disciples is for each one of us, but we do not pursue this mission alone. Discipleship is a calling of the body of Christ, and every member partners together in the work of the gospel. It is in and through local bodies of Christ that discipleship largely occurs. Our own discipleship relationships should be tethered to our churches. As we share the knowledge of God found in the Word of God with those we are discipling, we should personally be sitting under the preaching and teaching of our pastors and elders in our churches. We need to regularly gather with fellow believers to partake in the Lord's Supper, to be equipped and encouraged, and to receive accountability. Furthermore, it is in the context of a local body of Christ that people will see the gospel in action most clearly. Jesus said that all people will recognize followers of Christ by the love of Christ shared between them (John 13:35). While we can be recipients of God's love, we need the church to carry out His commands to one another. God's love, mercy, grace, generosity, and care are better communicated within a community of faith.

May we never forget that making disciples ultimately rests on God. It is dependent on the Spirit of God, not our eloquence, charisma, or talents, to enlighten minds to the truth of the gospel. No amount of effort on our end can make someone righteous; Christ alone declares someone justified before God, and He continues the work of growing us in His likeness. He alone brings new birth and new life in a person. Our role is to emulate Christ before a watching world. We are to put God's gracious work of justification and sanctification on display in our spheres of influence, attributing any good thing in us to Him. We adorn the gospel and trust in the gospel to transform hearts and minds. So yes, we assess our God-given gifts and abilities and seek to steward them well for the glory of God. Yes, we pray and consider where, when, and how we can strategically employ all that has been entrusted to us for the furtherment of His mission. Yes, we do this in partnership with our local churches. But ultimately, our hope in and for discipleship rests in Christ alone.

In your own words, write out the importance of discipleship.

_____

_____

_____

How should this discipleship relationship lead to other discipleship relationships in your life?

_____

_____

_____

While engaging in discipleship is a personal act of love and obedience to God, we do not have to do it alone. Are you involved in a local church? How can the local church help you in your personal evangelism and discipleship?

_____

_____

_____

"

We have been given a
body to be a part of — *one that
works better with us in it.*

"

Discipleship in the Local Church

As we have stated earlier in this study, a discipleship relationship is one in which a mature Christian is spending intentional time with a younger Christian, mentoring in the ways of the Christian life, incorporating Scripture, prayer, ministry, fellowship, and the pursuit of holiness. Some seasons and discipleship relationships will be formal, some will be informal, and some will last for longer seasons than others. The ideal environment for these relationships to take place is within the local church.

The local church is a beautiful gift God has given to His people, and one of the church's central missions is to be a place where the whole body grows together in Christlikeness (Ephesians 4:15-16). The church is a group of people united by the gospel and its members—repentant sinners, graciously redeemed by the blood of Christ, who strive each day to become more and more like Christ. Although discipleship is certainly possible outside the local church, the like-mindedness arising from covenant membership in the same local body will normally allow local church discipleship to be deeper and more efficient.

In our socially connected age, there are hundreds, even thousands of influencers fighting for our attention as we scroll through a feed. And so there can be a tendency to allow people at a distance to disciple us. The best of these may faithfully point us to the gospel and apply truths of Scripture in helpful ways. There is value in learning from popular preachers and tuning in to a podcast pointing us to gospel-living. But the reality of these digital, discipleship mediums is that those discipling you do not know you. They are not in the trenches with you, seeing both your good days and bad days. They cannot see your sin. They cannot see you in order to encourage you in righteousness. They do not have to learn to bear with you through your sin and love you through it—and neither do you have to do this for them. In other words, this type of relationship is easy and lacks the depth of relationship needed to gain spiritual maturity.

Discipleship in the local church allows for an authentic life-on-life community. The local church provides a family. A family is usually composed of different genders, different ages, different hobbies, and different likes and dislikes. It is diverse yet united. And within that family, all are able to know one another more intimately. Just as a family knows the ins and outs of every person in the household, so it is with the church. When you live with someone, you get to know that person in a deeper sense than if you were just an acquaintance—the good and bad habits, how to encourage and love that person, what makes him or her sad, and what triggers pain. This dynamic also exists within the local church. It is there that discipleship relationships thrive because members of your local church can see you, know you, be involved in your life, see how you live, and come alongside you and encourage you in the process of sanctification.

We have been given a body to be a part of—one that works better with us in it. In 1 Corinthians 12, Paul explains that the body has many members, and each member has an important role. In fact, Paul says that God has put the body together (1 Corinthians 12:24). If you are a part of one, take a look at your local church. God has given you to that body, and that body has been given to you. In your local body, you are to "have the same concern for each other. So if one member suffers, all the members suffer with it; if one member is honored, all the members rejoice with it" (1 Corinthians 12:25-26). The local body is a place where you can forgive and be forgiven, love and be loved, rebuke and be rebuked, encouraged and be encouraged, challenge and be challenged.

Walking alongside other believers in the local body can be hard and messy. Sin will be sure to creep in, and hurt can result from sin that is sometimes found within the local body. Do not let that be a deterrent from embracing the local church and becoming a part of one another. Allow these struggles to point you to the truth of the gospel. Discipleship does not suddenly make you sinless or a better Christian. Rather, through discipleship you are inviting someone into your life—over coffee, sharing a meal, taking a walk together, during a play date—to help you follow Jesus and reflect Him more faithfully as you flee from sin and run to the truth of the gospel.

Read 1 Corinthians 12. How is the local church a gift from the Lord to believers?

_____

_____

_____

_____

_____

If you are a part of a local church, how have you personally been blessed and encouraged through your local church body? If you are not part of a local church, what steps can you take toward finding one?

_____

_____

_____

_____

_____

Read Ephesians 4. What advantages do we find in these verses of living together within the body of Christ?

_____

_____

_____

_____

What are practical ways each one of you can open up your lives to one another so that you can spur one another along in your spiritual journey?

"

When we come to faith in Christ, we become *new creatures* who begin *growing in godliness* from that moment forward.

"

Discipleship is Long-Suffering

READ HEBREWS 10:19-25

Following Jesus is a lifelong pursuit. When we come to faith in Christ, we become new creatures who begin growing in godliness from that moment forward. Our commitment to growing in the faith is for all of life. God will finish the work of sanctification that He began in our lives, but we are invited and commanded to be invested in His work too (Philippians 1:6, 2:13). As we follow Jesus, both individually and in discipleship relationships, God equips us to remain steadfast throughout all of life.

Our sanctification, or becoming like Christ, is an on-going process that began when the Lord saved us and will continue until we see Him face-to-face. We grow in the faith as we study God's Word, spend regular time in prayer, and knit ourselves together in love with the body of Christ. In discipleship relationships, we can edify and be edified when we do these things together. As we grow together and remain connected to those who are invested in our growth, we will find the encouragement needed to press through hard times.

In Hebrews 10, the author lays out God's means of growth in our lives, closing with an exhortation to encourage one another in the faith more and more. In verses Hebrews 10:24-25, the author tells us to "watch out for one another to provoke love and good works, not neglecting to gather together, as some are in the habit of doing, but encouraging each other, and all the more as you see the day approaching." The command here is to "watch out for one another" so that we can "provoke love and good works." One translation calls us to "consider how to stir up one another to love and good deeds" (Hebrews 10:24 ESV). We are called to consider how to take stock and think of ways to encourage fellow believers to obey Christ and grow in affection for Him.

In order to obey these commands, we must be planted in a local body of believers so that people can invest in one another's lives. How can we encourage other believers to grow and flourish if we are not regularly connected to other believers?

In Hebrews 10:19, the author recounts his argument from the previous nine chapters, underscoring the truth that Jesus' sacrifice at the cross was enough to save us and enough to sanctify us. In paying for our sins at the cross, Jesus gave us free access to the Father through prayer. We do not have to go through priests to approach God, nor do we have to offer animal sacrifices for our sins. The work was finished by Christ who was both our Great High Priest and the Lamb of God who gave Himself for us. Through Him, we have access to God in prayer, the confession of our hope in Scripture, and sonship in the family of God. These gifts are the means by which we grow and persevere in the faith, both individually and corporately.

As you live a life of Christ-following, you will need encouragement from other believers more and more, not less and less. We never outgrow our need for relationships with our siblings in Christ. In regard to meeting together with believers, the author of Hebrews uses the phrase, "and all the more as you see the day approaching" (Hebrews 10:25). The day he is referring to is the return of Christ. So until we see Him, whether at His return or when He calls us home at the end of our life (whichever comes first), we are to keep holding fast to the means of encouragement Jesus made available to us at the cross. We continue in the things that help us grow, drawing from them increasingly more as we grow in maturity.

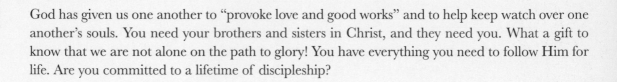

God has given us one another to "provoke love and good works" and to help keep watch over one another's souls. You need your brothers and sisters in Christ, and they need you. What a gift to know that we are not alone on the path to glory! You have everything you need to follow Him for life. Are you committed to a lifetime of discipleship?

Why does the author use the word "therefore" in verse 19 before moving to the practical exhortations for holding fast to the faith?

_____

_____

In Hebrews 10:24, the author exhorts us to prioritize gathering with other believers so that we can "watch out for one another to provoke love and good works." Take a moment to consider how to provoke love and good works in your discipleship partner or church members, and list some ideas.

_____

_____

_____

_____

Why is following Jesus in relationships with other believers vital to our growth?

_____

_____

Why might you need more (not less) connection to believers, prayer, and Scripture as you mature in the faith?

_____

_____

What hindrances have caused you to avoid or step away from discipleship in the past? How can you keep seeking the Lord with others in spite of those hindrances?

_____

_____

_____

PART TWO

The Gospel

> "The gospel is the *good news* that this Redeemer came, just as God said He would."

What is the Gospel?

Discipleship is a way of life for believers, and it is compelled and sustained by the gospel. So we have to ask: what is the gospel? The word "gospel" comes from the Greek word, *euaggelion*, and it simply means good news, glad tidings, or joyous message. In the New Testament, the gospel is the message of salvation by grace through faith in Jesus Christ, but this gospel is woven throughout Scripture. In fact, it is first noted in Genesis 3:15 when God addressed the serpent after Adam and Eve disobeyed God, and sin entered the world (also known as the fall). In the middle of the curse, God proclaimed the first promise of the gospel, a message of hope that rested on a redeemer. This message was and is good news for all mankind because the fall was not an isolated event. The introduction of human sin hurled all of humanity into sin (Romans 3:23), and the just penalty for any and all sin is death (Romans 6:23). This reality is what the Apostle Paul was referring to in Romans 5:12 when he said, "just as sin entered the world through one man, and death through sin, in this way death spread to all people, because all sinned." The gospel is the only remedy for this death. Beginning in Genesis, the anticipation for a future restoration is set in motion, and it rests on the person and work of Christ.

As the story of Scripture unfolds in the Old Testament, we see a progressive revelation of this plan of redemption. It is evident that God is and has always been active in history, working through real-life people and events to bring about the promised Redeemer. The gospel is the good news that this Redeemer came, just as God said He would. He came as a humble baby, born into the line of David. And this

God-man grew and lived a sinless life; He lived the life we could not live. Yet, as the prophets of old foretold, He died the death that our sins deserved on the cross. Though He knew no sin, He became sin so that His people might become the righteousness of God (2 Corinthians 5:21). But the story does not end there. Death could not hold Him down, and three days later, He was resurrected from the dead by the power of the Holy Spirit. He was who He said He was—the Messiah, the Anointed One, the Son of the living God. All who put their faith in Jesus Christ for salvation are united to Him, and we can be in a right relationship with God through our union with Christ. He took our sin, and by grace, we receive His righteousness. Through the death and resurrection of Jesus, we find life, not death.

And the story is ongoing today. While we can rest in the finished work of Christ, we also yearn for His return. We look forward to when Jesus will consummate His kingdom—where the presence of sin will be forever removed, God will make all things new, and He will dwell with His people again (Revelation 21:5). When we consider the biblical narrative, we can use the framework of creation, fall, redemption, and restoration/consummation to share the gospel. This presentation is helpful because it reminds us that the gospel is cosmic. All of creation was affected by sin. In fact, Romans 8 tells us that creation also waits with eager anticipation for this future consummation. The mark of sin taints the whole world, and so the gospel is good news for the entire universe!

WRITE OUT THE GOSPEL IN YOUR OWN WORDS USING THE PLOT MOVEMENTS:

Creation: _____

_____

Fall: _____

_____

Redemption: _____

_____

Restoration/Consummation: _____

_____

While the gospel is cosmic, it is also very personal. Each of us has a personal sin problem that requires a personal response to the person and work of Christ. Generally speaking, anyone can have an intellectual understanding of the contents of the gospel, but it is only by the Holy

Spirit that a person can believe in the gospel. This is why salvation is a gift; it is the Spirit who opens eyes to see the glory of Christ. The Spirit transforms hearts, renews minds, and enables belief. Regeneration and faith are possible only through God's saving and sustaining grace.

The gospel transforms individual hearts and lives. The gospel compels social and behavioral changes on both levels: corporate and individual. The gospel is the good news of Jesus Christ.

In Him, we are rescued from the wrath of God. In Him, our fellowship with God is restored. In Him, the power of sin in our lives is broken. In Him, we have the hope of future glorification where He will renew all things. He will usher in the new heaven and new earth, and we will forever be in the presence of Christ in resurrected bodies (see Revelation 21). What good news this is, indeed!

There are a few verses in Scripture that succinctly share the message of the gospel. Read 2 Corinthians 5:21, Romans 5:8, and 1 John 4:10. Then write out the gospel in 1-2 sentences.

_____

_____

_____

There is a difference between intellectually understanding the gospel and being transformed by the gospel. How has the gospel changed you?

_____

_____

Why is the gospel good news? Consider the implications of the gospel on a cosmic/corporate level and an individual level.

Cosmic/Corporate	Individual
Read: 1 Corinthians 15:3-4; Revelation 5:9, 21:1-2	*Read: Romans 8:1, 8:32; Ephesians 2:4-5*

"
The process of salvation
can be broken down into
three major elements:
justification, sanctification,
and glorification.
"

The Gospel at Work

The gospel is the good news of our salvation through faith in Jesus Christ. The process of salvation can be broken down into three major elements: justification, sanctification, and glorification. Within those elements are other aspects of discipleship like lordship and assurance. Understanding the order of our salvation is beneficial for a proper grasp of grace, faith, and works. It can be helpful to learn the terminology frequently used by Christians to describe our faith from beginning to end. Whether you are a new Christian or a seasoned saint, knowing the definitions of these words will aid you and your discipleship partner in your conversations about following Christ.

GLOSSARY OF TERMS ⟶

ELECTION

God's divine choice in the appointment to salvation for all those who would believe

God's election is based upon His gracious and sovereign will, not man's deeds. Before the foundation of the world, God set His love on His people. Because we were dead in our sins and unable to seek God, He sought us. In love, He predestined us for adoption as sons through Jesus Christ that we should be holy and blameless before Him and conformed into the image of Christ.

Passages to read together and consider:

Romans 8:29-30   Romans 9:11-12
Ephesians 1:4-6   2 Thessalonians 2:13

CALLING

God's sovereign drawing of sinners to salvation by grace through faith in Christ

God calls to Himself those whom He has appointed for salvation. The inward call of God is effectual, meaning it will produce faith in the hearts of the elect. Whereas many hear the gospel message (general calling), only those whom God has predestined for adoption will be drawn to Him through the invitation of the Holy Spirit (effectual calling).

Passages to read together and consider:

John 6:65   2 Thessalonians 2:14
2 Timothy 1:9   1 Peter 2:9
1 Peter 5:10

SALVATION

deliverance from sin and reconciliation to God through the life, death, and resurrection of Jesus

We are saved by grace through faith in Jesus Christ. We are saved from sin and to the kingdom of God when we repent from our sins and believe that Jesus died to pay for our sins. Salvation is freely offered to all who believe that Jesus is Lord and Savior who purchased our redemption with His own blood. Those who believe in Him will share an inheritance with Christ forever in heaven.

Passages to read together and consider:

John 1:12-13   John 3:16-18
Romans 5:8, 10   Romans 6:23

JUSTIFICATION

to be declared righteous before God

We are justified by grace alone through faith alone in Christ alone. We cannot make ourselves righteous before God, but He sent His own Son Jesus to live a perfect life, to die on the cross for our sins, and to be raised again with victory over sin, Satan, and death. His righteousness is imputed, or attributed, to all who believe in Him through faith.

Passages to read together and consider:

Romans 1:17   Romans 3:22-24
Galatians 2:16   Ephesians 2:8-9

LORDSHIP

submission to Christ's full authority over one's life

More than simply believing a set of facts about Jesus and salvation, lordship salvation acknowledges that we must yield our lives fully to Christ and His commands when we come to faith in Him. In belonging to Him, we are wholly committed to Him in every area of life. Complete submission to Him will be evidenced by good works as the fruit of real, saving faith.

Passages to read together and consider:

Luke 14:27   John 14:15
2 Corinthians 5:15   Galatians 2:20

SANCTIFICATION

to be made righteous or holy

From the moment believers come to faith in Christ, they are set apart for growth and maturity in Christ. They have been declared righteous positionally and are becoming righteous progressively through the work of the Holy Spirit who indwells them. Believers will continue in growth and holiness until they see Christ face-to-face.

Passages to read together and consider:

Romans 8:29   Philippians 1:6
1 Thessalonians 4:3   2 Thessalonians 2:13
1 John 3:2

GLORIFICATION

the final, sinless state of the believer in eternity with God

Our sanctification will be complete when Christ returns for His church, culminating in our glorified state wherein we will be perfect and sinless. Our bodies will be resurrected and renewed, and we will be like Christ, appearing with Him in glory.

Passages to read together and consider:

Romans 8:30   1 Corinthians 1:8
1 Corinthians 15:53   Philippians 3:20-21
Colossians 3:4

ASSURANCE

confidence that the saving work of Christ is sure and sufficient

Those who have repented of their sins and believed in the saving work of Christ for their reconciliation to God can have confidence that their souls are safe in Christ. All that Scripture requires is repentance and faith, both of which are gifts from God.

Passages to read together and consider:

John 5:24   John 10:27-29
1 John 1:9   1 John 5:12-13

QUESTIONS ⟶

Write the definitions for these terms in your own words. What similarities do you see in how they are accomplished? How are they different?

Election: _____

_____

Calling: _____

_____

Salvation: _____

_____

Justification: _____

_____

Lordship: _____

_____

Sanctification: _____

_____

Glorification: _____

_____

Assurance: _____

_____

Similarities: _____

_____

_____

_____

_____

_____

_____

Differences: _____

_____

_____

_____

_____

_____

How are both justification and sanctification accomplished by grace through faith?

_____

_____

_____

_____

Read Romans 8:28-30, and note Paul's use of the past tense in regard to our glorification. Knowing that we will not be glorified until we are with Christ, why might Paul have written about glorification as though it had already happened?

_____

_____

_____

_____

Have you ever struggled with assurance of your salvation? Read John 10:1-18. How does God's investment in your salvation encourage you?

_____

_____

_____

_____

"
The gospel changes
everything.
"

Life Worthy of the Gospel

The gospel changes everything. It is not just a heartwarming message that leads to our conversion. It is an enduring message of truth that radically changes our lives. For followers of Christ, it is a precious message of hope that sustains, comforts, and encourages. While our conversion is an instantaneous work of the Spirit where we are legally declared righteous in Christ, the result is a new life that involves a slow transformation into Christlikeness. Our salvation in many ways is past, present, and future. We are justified; our future glorification is secured, but our sanctification is progressive and occurs over a lifetime here on earth. But the truth remains—our lives ought to be different because we are different. We are united to Christ.

In light of our union with Christ, we are called to live in a manner worthy of the gospel of Jesus Christ. Paul urges believers to "live worthy of the calling" (Ephesians 4:1). He says it again in Philippians 1:27 when he says, "live your life worthy of the gospel of Christ." Those whom God has called into His kingdom are charged to "live worthy of God" (1 Thessalonians 2:12). But what does this kind of life look like? How does Scripture describe a life worthy of the gospel?

A life worthy of the gospel begins with a life transformed by the gospel. It begins with the work of the Spirit in us as He gives us a new heart and a new spirit (Ezekiel 36:26). When Christ reconciles us to Himself, He makes us a new creation (2 Corinthians 5:17). We are His workmanship (Ephesians 2:10). We are not only rescued from the penalty of sin, but we are free from the dominion of sin in our lives. We are given a new nature; we are given the capacity to live differently. So living a life worthy of the gospel is just that—living as a new creation in Christ. It is walking by the Spirit, not the flesh. It is walking by faith, not by sight.

Our new birth is a gift from God given to us by His saving grace. Our new life in Christ follows this new birth, and the beautiful truth is, it is completely dependent on His sustaining grace. However, this does not mean the Christian life is a passive life. Believers are called to walk by the Spirit and by faith, which implies an active response. The gospel not only offers eternity with Christ, but it also transforms our hearts. We are given new desires, and these new desires inevitably impact our behavior. The Spirit enables us to say no to the things of this world and our flesh and say yes to the things of God. Believers are now on this trajectory toward holiness, actively pursuing it in their everyday lives.

Living by the Spirit begins with knowing His Word. The Apostle Paul prays that the believers in Colossae would be "filled with the knowledge of His will" so that they would "walk worthy of the Lord, fully pleasing to Him" (Colossians 1:9-10). The word "filled" in this verse implies being wholly driven by the Word of God. He prays that they would grow in their knowledge of God to a degree that they would be compelled to live in accordance with it. This is a life pleasing to the Lord and worthy of the gospel, and this is how believers will bear fruit in every good work. When we faithfully walk, step by step, with the Spirit in obedience to His Word, we will see fruit in our lives. And as Jesus said in Matthew 7:15-20, our fruit reveals to whom we belong. It is our fruit that shows the world we are His disciples, and it is our fruit that glorifies God (John 15:8). This does not mean our salvation is something we can earn or achieve. No amount of good works or religiosity will save us. However, good fruit is evidence of our salvation. The indwelling Spirit in us is not powerless; He does not leave us unchanged in the here and now.

Living a life worthy of the gospel is also about abiding. We are grafted into the family of God by the grace of God, yet abiding proves that we are His disciples. So what does it mean to abide? Abiding means living out our union with Christ. Like a branch is connected and wholly dependent on the vine, we are connected to Christ and wholly dependent on Him. Our union with Christ means we have access to His strength, peace, love, and goodness. We are intricately tied to Him! Abiding is not based on who we are, but it is based on who He is. It is not about looking to our own strength and willpower to do better. Instead, it is about trusting in the Spirit's sanctifying work in us, submitting to His lordship. It is believing that He enables us to hold fast to Christ as Christ holds fast to us.

There is a beautiful dynamic between true believers and God on this side of heaven. As He supplies the grace and power to obey, we respond by obedience. We look to His Word for instruction on how to live, and He provides the wisdom and will to apply it to our lives. As He extends kindness to us, we repent which involves an active turning away from our sins and turning toward God. We put on the armor of God (Ephesians 6) which is provided to us for our protection against the world, the devil, and our flesh. We also pursue holiness by engaging in spiritual disciplines. We commune with God through prayer. We give thanks and worship Him with our lives because we find our deepest satisfaction, purpose, and joy in Him. We live as members of a local body of Christ, stewarding our gifts and resources for the common good. Our faith is in response to the work of the Spirit in our hearts. A life worthy of the gospel adorns the beauty and truth of the gospel.

Living a life worthy of the gospel is something we do in partnership with the Spirit. How does the work of God in your heart, soul, and mind impact how you live your day to day life?

_____

_____

_____

_____

Read Colossians 1:9-12 and 1 Peter 2:9-12. How do the apostles describe lives that are worthy of the gospel?

_____

_____

_____

In your own words, explain what it means to abide in Christ.

_____

_____

_____

_____

There are many ways to adorn the gospel with your life. What does this look like in your life right now? Take some time to pray, asking the Spirit to help you do this more and more.

"

All of Scripture testifies to the transcendent God who has *intimately worked in the details of human history* to accomplish our salvation.

"

Articulating Personal Testimony

What makes a good story? Most people would respond to that question with what they remember from an English literature class: interesting characters, compelling conflict, and a satisfying resolution. These elements are certainly essential for storytelling. However, it is also important to note that a good story is a testimony. A testimony is a witness or public declaration of truth. The details of a story or testimony work together to discover and prove something about the world. Therefore, storytelling has the ability to teach, inspire, and build.

The true storyteller is God Himself. God authored the greatest narrative in the universe, and through human authors, He has given this story through the Bible. All of Scripture testifies to the transcendent God who has intimately worked in the details of human history to accomplish our salvation. The smaller stories of the Bible are a part of God's larger plan for redemption. They culminate in the ultimate testimony of Jesus Christ, who lived, died, and rose from the grave so that we would be forgiven of our sins and have a relationship with God.

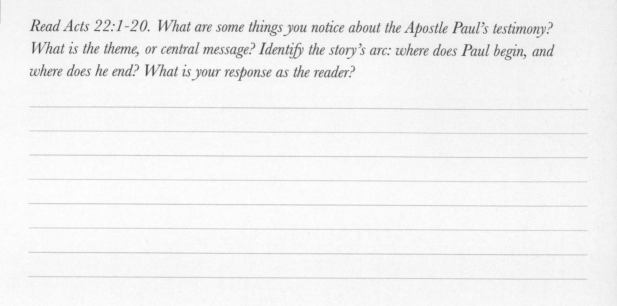

Read Acts 22:1-20. What are some things you notice about the Apostle Paul's testimony? What is the theme, or central message? Identify the story's arc: where does Paul begin, and where does he end? What is your response as the reader?

After being attacked by a mob and arrested in Jerusalem, Paul stood on the temple steps and declared his testimony before the crowd. Paul delivered his conversion story which was his transformation from chief persecutor of Christians to a prominent evangelist. Based on an encounter with Jesus, he testified to defend his mission in Jerusalem and glorify the redeeming power of God. Like Paul's testimony, our life's story also testifies to the saving work of Jesus. We can learn from Paul's boldness and gospel clarity to articulate our story.

Paul humbly looked at his past, realizing the depths of his sin. He did not allow shame to prevent him from boldly speaking about Jesus. A barrier to articulating personal testimony is shame. You may not feel like your story is dramatic enough. Even if you think your story is too clean or boring to make an impact, sin has still marked your life. Everyone has fallen short of God's standard and is in need of His saving grace (Romans 3:23). We and our world do not compare to the perfection of Jesus and the beauty of eternal paradise with Him. Or perhaps you feel humiliation over your past sins, memories of your old self continuing to haunt you. You cannot seem to shake the weight of regret. But you are a new creation in Christ (2 Corinthians 5:17). When you believed, you were clothed with the righteousness of Christ. When God looks at you, He sees His beloved child, not a wayward sinner. Satan will try to discourage you by reminding you of the past. But, you can take captive the memory and use it to testify to God's glory. You can boldly tell your story with graciousness toward yourself. A memory of the past is another opportunity to be thankful for the mercy of God and the new life you now have in Christ.

Describe your life before knowing Christ. What defined your identity? What did you pursue and value (materials, wealth, relationships, etc.)? What were the consequences? Recall thoughts, feelings, and environment to remember specific memories.

_____

_____

_____

_____

_____

_____

_____

Paul encountered the risen Jesus in a remarkable way. Radiating light from heaven, Jesus in His glory came near to him. In this way, Paul gave witness to the gospel—the death and resurrection of Jesus and its power to redeem. By the grace of God, the Holy Spirit still remarkably brings us into a knowledge of Christ. He peels back the scales from our eyes and reveals the kingdom of God to us. We were dead in our sins, but the Spirit of Jesus has made us alive through faith in Christ's righteousness (Romans 8:10). The Holy Spirit has made us aware of the life, death, and resurrection of Jesus for the salvation of God's people, and He propels us to believe this truth. In articulating our testimony, we should speak with gospel clarity to point others to Jesus.

Describe the moment you understood the gospel. What was the setting? How did you react to realizing your sin and God's plan to redeem you in Jesus? Identify a Scripture verse that captures the gospel.

_____

_____

_____

_____

_____

In the midst of sharing his testimony, Paul was bound in prison chains and staring at those who wanted to do him harm. Believing the gospel did not eliminate suffering from his life, but it did give him a mission, hope, and an eternal perspective. Material possessions, physical healing, and emotional or mental support may or may not be the result of believing in the gospel. These things are not promised. But, what is promised is our salvation from judgment and death. Because of the life, death, and resurrection of Jesus, we can live with freedom, gratitude, and joy. We have been forgiven of our sins, reconciled to God, and will spend eternity with Him in paradise. When we declare the supremacy of His name, we engage in God's redemptive work and invite the Holy Spirit to transform the hearts of our listeners.

In what ways have you experienced the transforming power of the gospel? Describe the new identity, hope, and perspective you have. How is God developing you to become more like Christ? How is God using you for His glory now?

_____

_____

_____

_____

_____

_____

_____

_____

_____

_____

Use the next page to write your full testimony.
Aim to keep the story under 10 minutes, and share it with your discipleship mentor.

MY TESTIMONY

"
You are not sent out
on your own. *You are equipped*
by the Holy Spirit.
"

Evangelism: Sharing the Gospel

Evangelism should be a natural outpouring of the good news of the gospel that has penetrated and changed our own hearts. Out of gratitude and awe that God would give His Son for a sinner, the redeemed person shares that good news with others. Through evangelism, we present the gospel to unbelievers in hopes that they will come to saving faith in Jesus Christ.

What is the gospel? When sharing your faith, it is essential to know and understand the gospel. Write out your understanding. As you think through what to say, remember to keep it clear and succinct. It can be helpful to reference a verse or passage to keep you on track.

Some may think that sharing the gospel is reserved only for pastors or missionaries, but it is not. Just as salvation is freely given to all who would believe, the message of the gospel should be shared by all who have freely received the gift of salvation. In Matthew 28:18-20, Jesus commands His disciples, "Go, therefore, and make disciples of all nations, baptizing them in the name of the Father and of the Son and of the Holy Spirit, teaching them to observe everything I have commanded you. And remember, I am with you always, to the end of the age." Jesus commands us to go and make disciples, and we do that by sharing the gospel with those who we encounter.

The approach to evangelism can vary, but the central message will remain the same. Sometimes the Lord may give you an opportunity to share with someone when you first meet, or that conversation may finally happen over a season of time in which you are getting to know another person and gaining trust so that he or she becomes willing to hear the gospel and how it changed your life.

There are many ways to live life, faithfully looking for opportunities to share the gospel. Sometimes work may feel tricky because you want to make sure you are not crossing boundaries with your co-workers, but you can be creative in your approach and live a life that loves them well and displays the love of Christ to them. For example, you can strike up a conversation in the breakroom at work, you can pray for a coworker who is going through suffering, and you can be the first to rejoice in a co-worker's promotion. Other areas in our lives such as restaurants, stores, our children's school, the soccer field, or even the waiting room can be places where we can begin to sow seeds of the gospel with whatever amount of time and conversations the Lord gives to us.

If someone asked you how to become a Christian, what would you say? Write some talking points that you would want to include in that conversation.

As you think about a conversation you would have with an unbeliever about coming to know Christ, spend some time thinking about objections and/or questions that they may have. How could you answer them?

OBJECTION/QUESTION	ANSWER

Sharing the gospel can be scary and intimidating. We can become overwhelmed because we do not feel equipped to share for fear of not having all of the answers. But it is important to remember that God has not called us to have all the answers; He has just called us to be faithful to share the good news. So it is okay to tell someone that you do not have an answer at that moment. Displaying honesty and authenticity in these situations speaks more loudly than stumbling through an answer that is later proven incorrect. Be vulnerable. Say you are unsure if you do not know, and trust the Spirit will use your faithfulness to share the gospel. And most importantly, be encouraged because God told us that He would be with us to the end of the age. You are not sent out on your own. You are equipped by the Holy Spirit.

Read Romans 10:14-17. Why must we share the gospel? Why is sharing the gospel urgent?

_____

_____

_____

_____

_____

Read these verses below. To what truth of the gospel does each verse point?

VERSE ⟶ GOSPEL TRUTH

Romans 3:10 _____

_____

Romans 3:23 _____

_____

Romans 6:23 _____

_____

Romans 5:8 _____

_____

Romans 10:9-10, 13 _____

_____

Romans 5:1-2 _____

_____

Romans 8:1 _____

_____

Spiritual Tips for Evangelism

- Be in the Word and pray daily.
- Have a clear understanding of the gospel.
- Be sensitive to the Spirit.
- Live a life of repentance, turning away from sin.
- Avoid gossip, and be of godly character in order not to taint your witness.
- Persevere in prayer and evangelism.
- Be a part of a Bible-believing local church. If possible, invite another member into your relationships with non-believers and partner to share the gospel together.
- Be content with your role. You may be used to plant a seed, while someone else waters it or sees it grow. Rejoice that you were used to share the gospel with another!

Relational Tips for Evangelism

- Ask good questions.
- Be a good listener. Focus on what they are saying, not what you want to say back.
- Be friendly. People do not like to feel like an evangelistic project. Be kind, and genuinely care about what they have to say.
- Observe body language.
- Speak kindly.
- Live godly lives. Your life and love will often trump what you say. Let it uphold your word and not disqualify it.
- Use what people say online as an opportunity to follow-up privately, in person.
- Do not be afraid to say "I don't know," and come back to someone.
- Be gracious, and do not assume you know what someone thinks or believes.
- Stay focused on the gospel instead of other differences like politics or schooling decisions.

BUT CHRIST BORE THE FULL WEIGHT
OF OUR SIN ON THE CROSS SO THAT
ALL WHO BELIEVE WILL RECEIVE
HIS RIGHTEOUSNESS.

For God loved the world in this way: He gave his one and
only Son, so that everyone who believes in him will not
perish but have eternal life.

John 3:16

OUR BROKENNESS AND SIN
NATURE SEPARATE US FROM
THE ONE TRUE, HOLY GOD.

for the wages of sin is death
Romans 6:23a

WHEN WE ACCEPT THE FREE
GIFT OF SALVATION, WE ARE
RECONCILED TO GOD AND
GIVEN ETERNAL LIFE.

But to all who did receive him, he gave
them the right to be children of God,
to those who believe in his name

John 1:12

The Whole Gospel

GOD

God created the world and everything in it. God, who is perfect, pure and good, created man and woman in His own image and designed us to live in perfect peace and intimacy with Him.

_____

Genesis 1:26-28

SIN

Mankind rebelled against God. Since the fall in Genesis 3, mankind became sinful by nature. Sickness, death, and brokenness were introduced into the world. Because of our sinful nature, we are cut off—separated from the one and only, perfect God.

_____

Genesis 3, Romans 3:23

RESPONSE

God calls us to repent of our sins and place our faith in Jesus, trusting in His perfect life, death, and resurrection. When we turn from our sins and believe the gospel, we are reconciled to God through His Son. God also gives us His Spirit to help us, guide us, and enable us to live godly lives. He promises that one day He will come again to make all things right, and we will live eternally with Him.

_____

Mark 1:15, Acts 20:21,
Romans 10:9-10, Acts 17:30, John 1:12

CHRIST

God provided a way for us to be right with Him again by sending His Son Jesus into the world. Jesus, who was fully God and fully man, lived a perfect, sinless life. He died on the cross for our sins and took on the full wrath that we deserve. In exchange, all who believe in Jesus will receive His righteousness and be at peace with God again. Jesus offered Himself up to the Father as the perfect sacrifice, fully able to pay the infinite depth that our sins owe. On the third day, He rose from the grave, declaring victory over death and sin.

_____

John 1:1, 3:16-17; 1 Timothy 2:5;
Hebrews 7:26; Romans 3:21-26, 4:25;
Acts 2:24; 1 Corinthians 15:20-22,
2 Corinthians 5:21

PART THREE

Bible Study and Scripture Memory

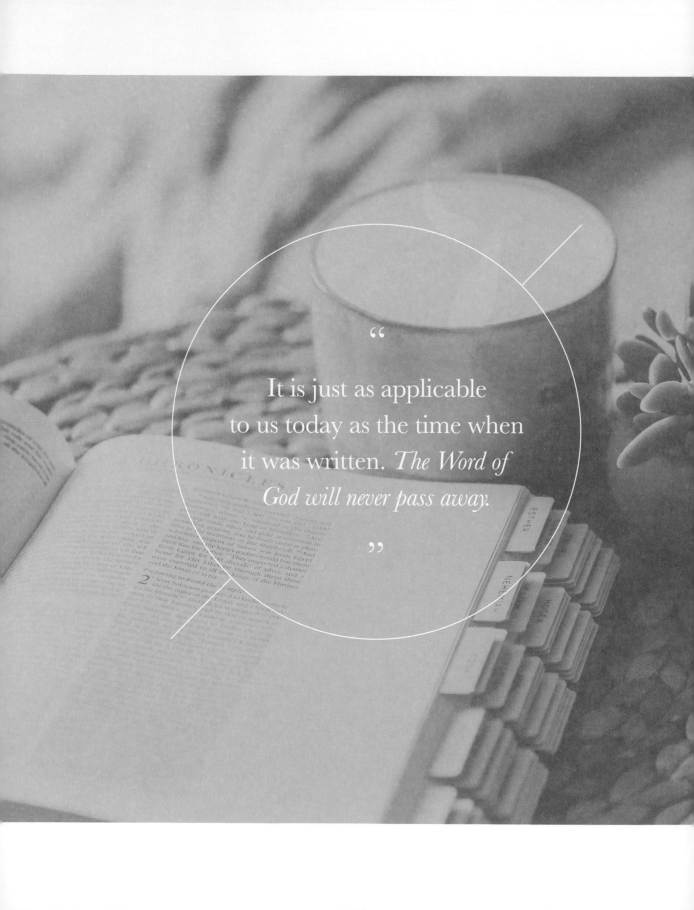

> " It is just as applicable to us today as the time when it was written. *The Word of God will never pass away.* "

We Need God's Word

WHAT IS THE BIBLE?

The Bible is not merely a book about God; it is the very Word of God. Our greatest aim in life is to know God and enjoy Him forever, and He has provided the means to do this through His Word. The Bible contains beautiful stories, prophecies, commands, and invitations to respond to the gospel. It begins by recounting the creation narrative when God spoke the world into existence and ends with a triumphant proclamation of Christ's return and victory over all. The main character and the hero of the story is Jesus, and all the Scriptures point to Him (Luke 24:25-27). It is inspired, inerrant, sufficient, and eternal.

The Bible is inspired, meaning that it is God-breathed (2 Timothy 3:16-17). It was written over a span of about 1500 years, using roughly forty different human authors. These authors were prophets, kings, fishermen, priests, doctors, and shepherds. Under the inspiration of the Holy Spirit, and using their unique personalities and writing styles, these men wrote exactly what God wanted them to write (2 Peter 1:20-21). Every word of Scripture is reliable and perfect. It is inerrant, meaning it is without error in the original manuscripts. It is completely trustworthy.

The Bible is also sufficient. For centuries, philosophers have pondered the deep questions of life: Why do I exist? What happens after death? Why is there suffering? Fortunately, God has provided everything we need to know for salvation and a life of godliness in His Word. The

Bible shows us not only how to be saved but also how to live lives honoring to Him. The Bible is eternal. Its truths are timeless and its wisdom boundless. We will never outgrow the Bible or our need for it. It is just as applicable to us today as the time when it was written. The Word of God will never pass away.

The Bible was given to us as a gift, and it is a bottomless treasure to those who love God. It tells us who God is and reveals His great love for us. Its truths bring life to our souls when we are weary and strengthen us when we are weak. It comforts us, challenges us, and spurs us on to greater obedience. It reminds us that we are not alone.

The Bible shows us how to be right with God. It tells us that we are not saved by doing enough good deeds, nor are we redeemed because we are in the top tier of morally virtuous humans around the world. Rather, the Bible shows us the standard of perfection required before a holy God, an achievement that only Jesus could attain. Through the words of Scripture, we come to an awareness of our sin and our need for a Savior. We are saved only through belief in Christ.

After we believe in Christ, Scripture tells us of our new identities. We were once enemies of God, but now we are His beloved children (John 1:12). We were once without hope, but now we are given an eternal and lasting inheritance and set on a mission with God (Matthew 28:16-20). Instead of determining truth based on our ever-changing emotions, we can look to the never-changing words of Scripture to remember that we are loved and adopted children of God, clothed with His righteousness. We no longer need to look to food, relationships, or a promotion at work to satisfy the deep longings in our souls; we have all that we need in Christ.

We learn that He will use every hardship and every unfulfilled longing for our good (Romans 8:28). Yet even after we are saved, we continue to sin. We forget our new identities as God's adopted children, forever loved and accepted in Him. Even then, the words of Scripture encourage us, remind us, rebuke us, and convict us of sin (2 Timothy 3:16-17).

The Bible tells us how to serve God and love others. Not only does the Bible tell us what actions to put off, but it also shows us a better way, revealing how to live pure and righteous lives in Christ. For example, as we open its pages, we are told to live without anger, rage, or filthy language and instead with humility, respect, and love (Colossians 3:1-17). As we meditate on God's Word, it changes our hearts and allows us to respond to the same circumstances in new and unexpected ways. The Bible equips us for every good work that God has prepared for us.

The Scriptures reveal wisdom for daily living. Often when we think of God's will, we crave a quick answer to practical decisions: Where should I go to school? What should I get for dinner? Should I buy this house? While the Bible does not give specific instructions on which coffee to buy at the grocery store or which spouse to choose, it does provide biblical wisdom for decision-making. As we spend time in Scripture, our minds are renewed. We learn biblical principles about how we should treat others, how to spend our money, and what to look for in a spouse. We find wisdom and blessing in following God's

Word and in applying biblical principles to specific circumstances in our lives.

The Bible teaches us and shows us what is true. In a world competing for our attention through a barrage of information and false teaching, it is important that we stand firm on the truth of God's Word. To those who love God, His words are sweet like honey. As we depend on Scripture in our personal lives and within our churches, our communities are strengthened. We are influenced less by the fluctuating culture, and we begin to look more like the unchanging One who made us. Our eyes are redirected from ourselves and onto our great God as we learn more about His all-sufficient love.

Has anyone ever taught you how to read the Bible? Discuss your history of studying the Bible together.

Look up 2 Timothy 3:16-17, Isaiah 55:10-11, and 1 Thessalonians 2:13. Why is studying the Bible important?

_____

_____

_____

In what ways do you feel ill-equipped to study the Bible? In what area of Bible study would you like to grow?

_____

_____

_____

Read Psalm 12:6, Romans 11:33, and 2 Peter 1:21. What do you learn about God's word from these verses?

_____

_____

_____

"
As we study the Bible,
we are called to do so
prayerfully and diligently.
"

Bible Study Methods

As we study the Bible, we are called to do so prayerfully and diligently (2 Timothy 2:15). To do this, we need God's help. Before studying Scripture, begin with prayer, asking the Spirit to open your eyes and help you to understand the text. Choose a Bible study method that helps you accurately understand the passage, both in its original meaning and in its application. This section will outline three methods for studying the Bible: the inductive method, Bible highlighting, and reading the Bible in a year.

#1 THE INDUCTIVE METHOD

One helpful tool to study the Bible is called the inductive method. The inductive method includes three primary components: observation, interpretation, and application. By studying Scripture in this order, we are able to better understand what the verses mean in context and more carefully apply them to our lives. For a more in-depth review of the inductive method, see the *Search the Word* resource from the Daily Grace Co.

BACKGROUND INFORMATION

Before we jump into the steps of this method, it is helpful to orient ourselves to the world in which the specific book of the Bible is set and written. Before studying any book of the Bible, it is worthwhile to read background information in order to understand the historical context in which the book was written. You could find this information in the introduction to each book of the Bible in the ESV Study Bible or in the *Bible Handbook* resource from the Daily Grace Co. In your reading, try to answer the following five archaeological questions:

1. Who is the author?

2. Who is the audience?

3. When was it written?

4. What is the purpose of the book?

5. What is the genre?

OBSERVATION/COMPREHENSION

During the observation section, we begin with the question, "What does the passage say?" To start, read the passage in context from start to finish. Many books of the Bible were intended to be read as a whole, and by reading the passage in context, we can better understand its original meaning. Reread the passage multiple times, and note key words such as:

• *Repeated words, phrases, and ideas.*

• *Transition words (i.e. therefore, because, likewise)*

• *Comparisons and contrasts*

• *Lists*

• *Unfamiliar words (look these up in the dictionary)*

Write down any questions you have about the text, which will be further examined in the interpretation phase.

Practice Using Philippians 1:1-11

Read the entire book of Philippians. Then reread Philippians 1:1-11, noting repeated words and phrases, transition words, and unfamiliar words. Write your observations below:

_____

_____

_____

_____

_____

_____

_____

_____

_____

_____

INTERPRETATION

Next, we begin to interpret Scripture, asking the question, "What does the passage mean?" In this phase, it is important to understand what the passage meant to its original audience before we apply it to our own lives. Complete the following steps to interpret the passage:

1. *Read other translations.*
2. *Read cross-references.*
3. *Summarize the passage.*
4. *Notice themes within the metanarrative of Scripture (creation, fall, redemption, restoration).*
5. *Look at trustworthy commentaries.*

Practice

Read Philippians 1:1-11 in multiple translations. How do these translations grow your understanding of the text?

_____

_____

_____

_____

_____

How would you summarize the passage?

_____

_____

_____

_____

_____

_____

_____

What themes do you notice within the metanarrative of Scripture (creation, fall, redemption, restoration)?

_____

_____

_____

_____

APPLICATION

Now that you have finished the important work of reading the passage in context and understanding its original meaning, we can begin to apply it to our everyday lives. If we skip the first two steps of comprehension and interpretation, we risk misinterpreting Scripture or taking verses out of context to suit our desires. In this section, we ask:

- *What attributes of God's character are revealed in the text?*
- *What do I learn about myself in light of who God is?*
- *How should this truth change me?*

Practice

What attributes of God's character are revealed in Philippians 1:1-11?

_____

_____

_____

What do you learn about yourself in light of who God is?

_____

_____

_____

How can you apply the truths of this passage to your life?

_____

_____

_____

_____

_____

_____

_____

Bible highlighting is another helpful tool in studying Scripture and helps us to read the Bible slowly, noting key words and ideas. As we read, we highlight God's attributes and notice key themes throughout the passage. For a more in-depth review of Bible highlighting, see the *Bible Highlighting Guide* from the Daily Grace Co.

Here is an example from Ephesians 2:1-10 using the following highlighting key:

SAMPLE HIGHLIGHTING KEY

Yellow = Character of God

Blue = Redemption

Green = Commands to Obey

Orange = Nature of Man/Flesh + Sins to Avoid

Purple = Book-Specific Key Themes

Pink = Verses to Memorize

Ephesians 2:1-10

And you were dead in your trespasses and sins in which you previously walked according to the ways of this world, according to the ruler of the power of the air, the spirit now working in the disobedient. We too all previously lived among them in our fleshly desires, carrying out the inclinations of our flesh and thoughts, and we were by nature children under wrath as the others were also. But God, who is rich in mercy, because of his great love that he had for us, made us alive with Christ even though we were dead in trespasses. You are saved by grace! He also raised us up with him and seated us with him in the heavens in Christ Jesus, so that in the coming ages he might display the immeasurable riches of his grace through his kindness to us in Christ Jesus. For you are saved by grace through faith, and this is not from yourselves; it is God's gift—not from works, so that no one can boast. For we are his workmanship, created in Christ Jesus for good works, which God prepared ahead of time for us to do.

Practice

Use the sample highlighting key to highlight Philippians 1:1-11 provided on the next page.

Philippians 1:1-11

Paul and Timothy, servants of Christ Jesus: To all the saints in Christ Jesus who are in Philippi, including the overseers and deacons. Grace to you and peace from God our Father and the Lord Jesus Christ. I give thanks to my God for every remembrance of you, always praying with joy for all of you in my every prayer, because of your partnership in the gospel from the first day until now. I am sure of this, that he who started a good work in you will carry it on to completion until the day of Christ Jesus. Indeed, it is right for me to think this way about all of you, because I have you in my heart, and you are all partners with me in grace, both in my imprisonment and in the defense and confirmation of the gospel. For God is my witness, how deeply I miss all of you with the affection of Christ Jesus. And I pray this: that your love will keep on growing in knowledge and every kind of discernment, so that you may approve the things that are superior and may be pure and blameless in the day of Christ, filled with the fruit of righteousness that comes through Jesus Christ to the glory and praise of God.

Another fruitful way to study the Bible is to read the Bible in a year. By reading several chapters of Scripture a day, you are able to understand the big themes of the Bible and see that all of Scripture points to Jesus. It can be helpful to choose a reading plan such as *The Story of Redemption* from the Daily Grace Co. to stay on schedule throughout the year. As you read, note the key themes of creation, fall, redemption, and restoration.

Discussion

- *Have you ever read through the entire Bible?*
- *Which Bible study method do you prefer and why? Discuss the Bible study methods you have used in the past.*
- *Discuss the benefits and differences of the three methods described, as well any remaining concerns you have about personal Bible study.*

"

The *questions we ask* when studying the Bible can largely determine what we gather from it.

"

Asking Intentional Application Questions

Asking good questions is vital to our understanding of the Scriptures and our growth as disciples. The questions we ask when studying the Bible can largely determine what we gather from it. Whichever method we choose to approach in our time of studying God's Word, it is important that we position ourselves with curiosity and humility, not seeking our own agendas but searching for ways to know and love God more. We can be more intentional with how we apply God's Word by asking these four overarching questions as we read the text:

1. *What does this passage teach me about God?*

2. *What does this passage teach me about mankind?*

3. *What does this passage teach me about how mankind should respond to God?*

4. *What does this passage teach me about how to respond to others?*

I. WHAT DOES THIS PASSAGE TEACH ME ABOUT GOD?

God is the main character of the Bible. Every aspect of Scripture speaks of Him and reveals something about who He is, even if it is not explicitly stated. We can easily jump to inserting ourselves or looking for ways to connect the passage to our present circumstances. However, we should always begin our interpretation by searching for what we can learn about God in the text. Our understanding of who He is shapes our understanding of everything else.

- *What attributes of God does the passage reveal?*
- *What does it teach us about His character?*
- *What do we learn about His cares and concerns?*
- *What does He love or hate?*
- *How does He respond to His people?*
- *What does it reveal about His redemptive plan?*
- *What promises does He make?*
- *Do you see the full work of the Trinity displayed?*

Asking these types of questions brings God to the forefront of our study. Reading the Bible becomes less about connecting it to our circumstances and more about knowing God and understanding more about Him and His purposes.

---

2. WHAT DOES THIS PASSAGE TEACH ME ABOUT MANKIND?

In the Biblical narrative, Scripture speaks of the role of mankind. Mankind is created in the image of God and at the center of His plan and purpose. When studying the pages of the Bible, we should be thinking through what each passage teaches us about our identity. We can understand ourselves better by asking questions like:

- *How does this passage help us to understand mankind as image-bearers?*
- *How does it reveal our fallen nature?*
- *What does it teach us about living as people who are redeemed in Jesus Christ?*

3. WHAT DOES THIS PASSAGE TEACH ME ABOUT HOW MANKIND SHOULD RESPOND TO GOD?

The study of God and the study of mankind lead us directly to how we should respond to Him. We are made in His image, but there are elements of His character that are true only of Him. The Bible speaks of His majesty (1 Chronicles 29:11), authority (Romans 13:1), and sovereignty (Psalm 115:3). The Bible speaks of our fallen nature (Romans 5:12), the hope offered to us (Romans 6:23), and the purpose for our lives (Matthew 22:37). Considering both natures, we can ask questions like:

- *How does this passage lead us to praise and worship God?*

- *How does it lead us to confess and repent of sin in our lives?*

- *How does it lead us to revere and obey God?*

---

4. WHAT DOES THIS PASSAGE TEACH ME ABOUT HOW TO RESPOND TO OTHERS?

God created us to be in community. When God brings us into a relationship with Himself, we are also brought into His family. God's family, united under the banner of the gospel, becomes a beacon of hope and light to a watching world. The Bible has a lot to say about how God intends for us to act toward one another. We are wise to ask questions when considering what a passage is teaching us about how to respond to others in light of what we have learned.

- *How does this passage help me to consider my relationships?*

- *In what ways does it encourage me to love, serve, and care for others?*

- *In what ways does it teach me about my role in the body of Christ?*

APPLICATION PRACTICE ⟶

Practice *Read Romans 5:1-5, and use the four overarching questions to apply the passage:*

What does this passage teach me about God? _____

_____

What does it teach me about mankind? _____

_____

How should mankind respond to God? _____

_____

How should mankind respond to others? _____

_____

Fleshing out the implications of a passage does not always come easy. We often search for tangible applications that we can put into action. Some passages have direct commands, and asking certain questions can bring out clear answers to how we should respond to what we have read.

- *Is there a command to obey?*   • *Is there a promise to claim?*
- *Is there an example to follow?*   • *Is there a sin to avoid?*

Practice *Read Colossians 3:1-17, and use the questions listed above to apply the passage.*

_____

_____

_____

_____

_____

_____

_____

_____

_____

_____

_____

Other passages are not as straightforward. However, asking broader, all-encompassing questions can lead us to look at our hearts and how God might be using the text to bring attention to how we think or what we believe.

- *What does God want me to understand from this passage?*
- *How should this truth shape my desires?*

- *What does this passage expose about my own heart?*
- *How does my response reveal underlying beliefs?*
- *How should this understanding transform the way I live?*

Delving into Scripture by asking intentional questions helps encourage us to approach God's word with an eagerness to learn from it. God's Word abounds in answers and should transform and shape the way we live. By asking good questions, we position ourselves for the Holy Spirit to guide our understanding and conform us into the likeness of Christ.

What is your usual approach to asking questions when studying the Bible? Why is it important that we ask good questions?

Discuss which questions stuck out most to you and why?

Write a prayer, and ask God to prepare you for studying His Word with curiosity, humility, and eagerness to learn from it. Pray this regularly as you approach God's Word.

"
Scripture memory helps
us remember *who God is.*
"

Why Memorize Scripture?

We have discussed both the importance of knowing God's Word for life and godliness as a believer. One of the ways in which we cement these truths into our hearts and minds is through Scripture memory. Deuteronomy 11:18 exhorts us, "Imprint these words of mine on your hearts and minds, bind them as a sign on your hands, and let them be a symbol on your foreheads." Scripture memory is the discipline and practice of committing Scripture to memory, storing up the Word of God in our hearts. Whether a few passages, a single verse, or an entire book, there is so much value in taking intentional time to memorize Scripture.

Jesus frequently quoted Scripture to His disciples and the crowds He taught. In Scripture, Jesus is recorded to have quoted from the Old Testament roughly 180 times. Jesus' use of Scripture points to the authority of the Word of God. Calling Scripture to mind can serve us in a myriad of ways. 2 Timothy 3:16-17 says, "All Scripture is inspired by God and is profitable for teaching, for rebuking, for correcting, for training in righteousness, so that the man of God may be complete, equipped for every good work." Let us look specifically into the importance and necessity of embracing a discipline of Scripture memory in our lives.

Scripture memory helps us to remember who God is and what He promises to His people. We are a people prone to wander and forget. In one moment we rejoice in God's faithfulness to us, while doubting and questioning Him in the next. When life seems unkind and unfair, remembering Scripture can point us outside of our present circumstances to the sovereign God of the Bible who we can continually trust and rely on. It reminds us of His unchanging character and His promises, even when all around us seems to be shifting and unstable.

Read the following verses/passages. Share an example for each of how committing them to memory can help you remember who God is and what He promises to His people:

PSALM 100:5 _____

DEUTERONOMY 31:8 _____

PROVERBS 3:5-6 _____

Scripture memory helps us fight sin. We can be flooded by emotions, circumstances, or temptations that provoke us to respond. In these instances, we can give little credence to discernment and patience, and instead, we want to instantly gratify the desires that can lead us into sin. But Scripture helps us to combat the temptation to give in and equips us to stand firm. The psalmist shared from experience, "I have treasured your word in my heart so that I may not sin against you" (Psalm 119:11). The more we read and memorize Scripture, the more readily accessible it is to us throughout our days when we do not have our Bible on hand. When we need it most to override the desires of our flesh, Scripture memory helps us to access the truth and instruction of God in any given situation. The Bible does not speak specifically into every circumstance, but it does instruct and equip us in every way to live godly lives. Therefore, we are better equipped to wage war with sin when memorizing Scripture.

Read the following verses/passages. Share an example for each of how committing them to memory can help you fight sin:

PROVERBS 15:1 _____

PHILIPPIANS 2:3-4 _____

I THESSALONIAN 2:4 _____

Scripture memory helps us to encourage and exhort others. There will be countless opportunities for us to speak into the lives of others, whether in bearing one another's burdens, holding others accountable, comforting them, or building them up. The greatest words we can offer to someone are not our own but those inspired by God and recorded in the pages of the Bible. God's word is powerful and never returns void of its purpose. It heals and rebukes, and it corrects and calms all the same. Quoting Scripture as a means of encouraging, or exhorting, lends us to speak with God's authority and purpose into the life of another instead of our own.

Read the following verses. Share an example for each of how committing them to memory can help you encourage and exhort others?

PSALM 34:18 _____

I JOHN 1:9 _____

I CORINTHIANS 10:31 _____

Scripture memory equips us to share and defend the gospel. We will undoubtedly be presented with opportunities to share the hope we have found in Jesus Christ. When we struggle to explain the saving work of the gospel, we can memorize Scripture that helps us to better articulate it. There are numerous passages of Scripture that help us to clearly explain salvation in Christ. Additionally, sharing passages of Scripture can embolden us with confidence, knowing that the power and authority are coming from God's Word and not our own. If questions are posed or if attacks follow, Scripture prepares us to defend what we believe to be true. By memorizing Scripture, we can better offer answers and evidence for the truth about God and the work of the gospel in our lives.

Read a few of the listed verses of Scripture that clearly share the gospel message, and see if you can add any. Choose one you can strive to commit to memory:

ROMANS 6:23 _____
ISAIAH 53:5 _____
2 CORINTHIANS 5:21 _____
TITUS 3:4-7 _____
I JOHN 4:10 _____
I PETER 2:24-25 _____

Ultimately, the goal of Scripture memory is that our hearts and minds would be transformed by the Word of God flowing out into our daily words and actions. Saturating ourselves in the Scriptures provides us with wisdom and discernment to combat the many voices seeking to oppose or falsify God's Word. Romans 12:2 reminds us, "Do not be conformed to this age, but be transformed by the renewing of your mind, so that you may discern what is the good, pleasing, and perfect will of God." There is much of this world that will speak against the truth of Scripture; we are better equipped to sift through the noise by implanting God's Word deep within our hearts.

The main hope and
goal of Scripture memory
is to *plant God's Word*
deep in our hearts.

Scripture Memory Methods

There are a variety of ways and methods by which we can commit Scripture to memory. As you become more comfortable with which ways work best, you can get creative and innovative with how you will choose to exercise this discipline. Additionally, find accountability with a friend or mentor who can regularly check in and test your progress in memorizing Scripture. Clearly communicate your goals, and schedule a time to check in with one another.

Two important aspects of Scripture memory are repetition and familiarity. The more you see, read, or hear something, the more it will become ingrained in your memory. <u>One of the most simple methods that will serve you well is reading the same verse or passage over and over.</u> This can be something you add into your morning or nightly routine. You can even read it over as you wash the dishes, go for a walk, or wait in line to pick your children up from school. Little margins in your day provide the perfect spaces to read over your Scripture memory verse a few times. You will be surprised how quickly you can remember it on your own!

To keep track of the verses you are memorizing or practicing, it is helpful to write them out in a spiral-bound notebook or on index cards to keep in a box. Having a Scripture memory library of sorts will allow you to go back to verses or passages over time and continue memorizing them, even after you have mastered memory the first time. It would be helpful if there is a way to make it portable. You can leave this in your car, on your nightstand, or in a backpack or purse to reference throughout your days. Having it close by allows you to access it when you have moments in your day to do so. It also keeps it visible to remind you to keep practicing.

(2) — **Another method that can be used for a single verse or even larger paragraphs is to write out the first letter of each word.**

EXAMPLE:

"Trust in the LORD with all your heart, and do not rely on your own understanding; in all your ways know him, and he will make your paths straight." Proverbs 3:5-6

T i t L w a y h,
a d n r o y o u;
i a y w k h,
a h w m y p s.
P 3:5-6

This method serves as a guide to the passage, giving you the clue to each word of the verse with a letter. It also helps to include punctuation, capitalization, and verse reference, which also give clues to memorizing as accurately as possible. You can write the letters on your wrist, create a lock screen for your phone, or write them on a sticky note each day. The first letter method can even be helpful for memorizing an entire chapter of a book. Once you feel that you have confidently mastered one passage, you can continue to add on the letters of the next verse. Before you know it, you will be able to recite and share an entire book of the Bible from memory.

(3) — **A similar method can be found in using a whiteboard or chalkboard.** You begin this method with a full written verse or passage. Take a week to read over it multiple times each day to grow in familiarity. For the second week, begin by erasing a few words from the board. When you come back to it each day, see if you are able to fill in the words by memory. If you are not able to do this, refer back to the original verse for help, but once you are able to recite the verse with only a few words missing, erase a few more. Continue the process until you can erase the entire board. For your last week, spend each day re-writing the entire verse completely by memory.

HERE'S AN EXAMPLE TO HELP YOU GET STARTED:

"Trust in the LORD with all your heart, and do not rely on your own understanding; in all your ways know him, and he will make your paths straight." Proverbs 3:5-6

"Trust in the _____ with all your _____, and do not rely on your own _____; in all your _____ know him, and he will make your _____ straight." Proverbs 3:5-6

A final suggestion, although this list is not exhaustive, is to put your memorization to music. God created our minds with individuality, and for some of us, song lyric memory comes with ease. We might hear a song a few times on the radio before we know it by heart. The same can be done for Scripture memory. There are numerous artists who have curated Scripture memory albums for purchase by taking passages of Scripture and putting them to music. But, of course, you can do this on your own by making up an original tune or even adding words to an instrumental piece. Once you have a Scripture memory song, aim to sing it while getting ready in the mornings or while driving to the grocery store.

Whichever method best suits you, remember the main hope and goal of Scripture memory is to plant God's Word deep in our hearts. We will assuredly be blessed and encouraged by the time we give to soaking up the truth of Scripture in a way that allows us to remember and reference it in times of need.

 What potential roadblocks do you see in your discipline of Scripture memory?

_____

_____

How can you be challenged and encouraged in this area?

_____

_____

What methods do you find most helpful to you?

_____

_____

Discuss and make a plan for memorizing Scripture.
- *What verse/passage will you memorize?*
- *Why do you want to memorize this passage/verse?*
- *What method will you use?*
- *How will you be held accountable for your Scripture memory progress?*

Scripture Memory Tracker

Use these pages to document your progress
in memorizing Scripture.

- ☐ Begin with the date you start memorizing a certain
  verse or passage of Scripture and the method
  you will be using.

- ☐ Write the verse or passage in its entirety, and include the
  version of Scripture you are reciting after the reference
  (ex. Proverbs 3:5-6 CSB, Proverbs 3:5-6 ESV).

- ☐ Briefly share why you chose this specific verse or
  passage as a means of remembering the importance
  of the truth it holds.

- ☐ Follow up regularly with a friend or a mentor to
  practice what you have memorized.

- ☐ Continue doing this even after you have committed
  the verse or passage to memory, and keep it fresh
  on your mind.

- ☐ Once you feel that you have memorized the verse or
  passage in its entirety, write down the date you
  committed it to memory.

START DATE: / / METHOD USED: _____

Scripture to Memorize: _____

_____

_____

_____

_____

Why I chose this Scripture to memorize: _____

_____

Follow Up ○ ○ ○ ○ ○ ○ ○ ○ ○   Date Committed to Memory: _____

START DATE: / / METHOD USED: _____

Scripture to Memorize: _____

_____

_____

_____

_____

Why I chose this Scripture to memorize: _____

_____

Follow Up ○ ○ ○ ○ ○ ○ ○ ○ ○   Date Committed to Memory: _____

START DATE: / / METHOD USED: _____

Scripture to Memorize: _____

_____

_____

_____

_____

Why I chose this Scripture to memorize: _____

_____

Follow Up ○ ○ ○ ○ ○ ○ ○ ○ ○   Date Committed to Memory: _____

START DATE: / /   METHOD USED: _____

Scripture to Memorize: _____

_____

_____

_____

_____

Why I chose this Scripture to memorize: _____

_____

Follow Up ○ ○ ○ ○ ○ ○ ○ ○ ○   Date Committed to Memory: _____

START DATE: / /   METHOD USED: _____

Scripture to Memorize: _____

_____

_____

_____

_____

Why I chose this Scripture to memorize: _____

_____

Follow Up ○ ○ ○ ○ ○ ○ ○ ○ ○   Date Committed to Memory: _____

START DATE: / /   METHOD USED: _____

Scripture to Memorize: _____

_____

_____

_____

_____

Why I chose this Scripture to memorize: _____

_____

Follow Up ○ ○ ○ ○ ○ ○ ○ ○ ○   Date Committed to Memory: _____

START DATE: / / METHOD USED: _____

Scripture to Memorize: _____

_____

_____

_____

_____

Why I chose this Scripture to memorize: _____

_____

Follow Up ○ ○ ○ ○ ○ ○ ○ ○ ○　　Date Committed to Memory: _____

START DATE: / / METHOD USED: _____

Scripture to Memorize: _____

_____

_____

_____

_____

Why I chose this Scripture to memorize: _____

_____

Follow Up ○ ○ ○ ○ ○ ○ ○ ○ ○　　Date Committed to Memory: _____

START DATE: / / METHOD USED: _____

Scripture to Memorize: _____

_____

_____

_____

_____

Why I chose this Scripture to memorize: _____

_____

Follow Up ○ ○ ○ ○ ○ ○ ○ ○ ○　　Date Committed to Memory: _____

PART FOUR

A Life of Prayer

"
In conjunction with Scripture,
prayer is one of the primary
ways for Christians to *know
and experience God.*
"

Understanding Prayer

In any relationship, communication is of utmost importance. How can we grow in our love for a spouse or our care for a friend if we never talk to them? The same is true in the Christian's relationship with God. In conjunction with Scripture, prayer is one of the primary ways for Christians to know and experience God. Prayer can be simply defined as talking to God. We can speak to God anytime and anywhere. We have been given the priceless gift of direct access to God through the sacrifice of Jesus. Not only that, but we are encouraged in Scripture to approach God with confidence, knowing that we will find mercy and grace when we need it.

Prayer can feel hard sometimes, and we get discouraged and distracted easily. Looking at the biblical commands and examples of prayer can help us understand why we should pray and how to do it. The Lord always equips us to obey His commands, and when it comes to the commands to pray, He has given us everything we need to talk to Him.

WHY PRAY?

From Genesis to Revelation, we see God's people crying out to Him in prayer. Whether it is praise for God's greatness, confession of sins, supplication for help, lament for rebellion, gratitude for God's intervention, or intercession for others—we see all different kinds of prayer commanded and displayed in Scripture.

In the Old Testament, the people often relied on prophets, judges, priests, or kings to intercede for them. But when Jesus came and died for our sins at the cross, He gave us the ability to pray to God ourselves without the need for a priest or a prophet because Jesus Himself is our mediator. We have been given a gift that the saints of old could not have imagined: free access to the Father at any time. We should pray because it is a privilege to do so. The ability to freely speak to our holy God was bought at the cross with Jesus' blood.

God speaks to us through His Word, and we speak back to Him through prayer. Often, we will find it helpful to pray as we read Scripture. In this way, we converse back and forth with the Father and grow in our knowledge of and love for Him. Prayer keeps us tethered to His side throughout the day and reminds us how needy we are for Him to work in our lives and in the lives of others. God is pleased to move and work in our lives when we pray.

CHRIST'S EXAMPLE AND ENCOURAGEMENT

Jesus teaches us how to pray in the Sermon on the Mount in Matthew 6:9-15, but He also modeled prayer to the Father. He was known to slip away from crowds and seek God in quiet, isolated places. If Jesus, who is God's Son, thought it beneficial to devote time to prayer, how much more do we? Jesus assumed that His followers would pray, too. Just before demonstrating how to pray in the Sermon on the Mount, Jesus gives instructions using the phrase, "when you pray," three times—not if you pray, but when. His assumption is that His disciples, including His followers today, would pray.

If that was not enough, we have the promise from Scripture that Jesus, who is now seated at the right hand of the throne of God in heaven, still intercedes for us. We never pray alone because both Jesus and the Holy Spirit are praying with and for us, taking our prayers and making them better—even when we do not know exactly what to pray.

COMMANDS TO PRAY

Scripture exhorts us not just to pray but to pray often. God knew we would struggle to be faithful in prayer, so He reminds us often in His Word to stay in communion with Him through conversation. Undergirding many of the prayers in the New Testament are requests for believers to grow in their knowledge of God. We can combat prayerlessness and grow in the knowledge of God with obedience to these commands:

- *"Pray at all times in the Spirit with every prayer and request, and stay alert with all perseverance and intercession for all the saints"* (Ephesians 6:18).

- *"Don't worry about anything, but in everything, through prayer and petition with thanksgiving, present your requests to God. And the peace of God, which surpasses all understanding, will guard your hearts and minds in Christ Jesus"* (Philippians 4:6-7).

- *"Devote yourselves to prayer; stay alert in it with thanksgiving"* (Colossians 4:2).

- *"pray constantly, give thanks in everything; for this is God's will for you in Christ Jesus"* (1 Thessalonians 5:17-18).

God's commands are always for our good. In calling us to be steadfast in prayer, God is not burdening us but is giving us a way to relieve our burdens. In kindness, He has made a way for us to call on Him at any moment. When we obey, we will find exactly what we need. As the author of Hebrews encourages us, "Therefore, let us approach the throne of grace with boldness, so that we may receive mercy and find grace to help us in time of need" (Hebrews 4:16).

Why is it such a privilege to draw near to God in prayer? Read Hebrews 10:19-22, and list the reasons prayer is a gift from God.

_____

_____

_____

Read Matthew 14:23, Mark 1:35, and Luke 5:16. What can we learn from Jesus' patterns of prayer?

_____

_____

Read Matthew 6:5-15. List some observations about prayer from Jesus' teaching and example.

_____

_____

_____

Read Romans 8:26-27. What is the Holy Spirit's involvement in our prayer life? How does that encourage you to pray?

_____

_____

Read Hebrews 7:25 and Romans 8:34. What is Jesus' involvement in your prayer life? How does that encourage you to pray?

_____

_____

"
Draw *away* from
life's distractions and
draw *near* to God.
"

Private Prayer

The quiet and solitary life of a monastery cultivates an atmosphere for devoted religious observance. Monks, who withdraw from society in order to deny worldly indulgences, are able to pursue spiritual disciplines with intensity. From sunrise to sunset, they spend many hours in liturgy, a structure of worship allowing for a deep dive into private prayer. But, with family obligations, work, and other ministerial demands, most believers are not able to adhere to a strict schedule of monastic practices. From social media to the latest news headline, our modern world presents distractions that pull our attention away from God. We navigate a chaotic world full of noise and confusion. The silence of a monastery is difficult to replicate in our own environments. Still, Christians are called to develop a private prayer life for growing in our relationship with God. Striving toward the image of our Savior, we can look to Jesus who, though He was completely focused on His earthly mission, made time to commune with His Father privately. We can create a liturgy of private prayer that fits where we are in life yet challenges us to draw away from life's distractions, and draw near to God.

PRAYING ALONE

Praying alone is an important aspect of a private prayer life. Communal prayers during church services are also vital, but in these settings, it is easy to let your heart and mind wander as you listen to the prayer of the pastor or service leader. We are not able to strengthen our personal relationship with God if we are only reliant on corporate prayer. Since we are susceptible to drift as we converse with God, praying alone develops the skill of presence. Being present in prayer is calling to mind the nearness of a Holy God. The reality that the God of the Universe has allowed sinners like us to approach

His throne through the saving work of Jesus is a truth that evokes total engagement and focus. Alone, we are forced to come face to face with ourselves as we come face to face with the radical love of God in Jesus. This type of prayer is incredibly intimate and vulnerable.

In Matthew 6:5-8, Jesus commands us to pray privately, and when we do so, Jesus says the Father sees us. The Holy Spirit is with us and assures us that the Father is receiving our petitions. In private prayer, there is no temptation to babble (Matthew 6:7) for others' attention and approval. We can rest before the Lord in silence and stillness, knowing that God knows the issues of our hearts. Luke 5:16 says that Jesus "often withdrew to deserted places and prayed." Our Lord and Savior prayed for extended periods of time in solitude and quiet. Jesus displayed the depth of His intimacy with the Father and His reliance on God to be equipped for ministry. Jesus was the perfect and eternal Son of God who still sought to refresh His human nature through solitary prayer. How much more do we need to seek the Lord's face through this spiritual discipline? Even though it will be difficult to unplug from life at first, we can trust that in private prayer, our souls will find nourishment and strength to carry out our God-given tasks.

PRAYING ONE ON ONE

Private prayer can also be performed between two people. Our human relationships thrive when we share life's joys and challenges. God receives glory when we reflect the love He has shown us, and privately praying with another is a way we love our neighbor. Hearing the sin issues of our prayer partner, we empathize and help carry burdens (Galatians 6:2) as Christ carried our sins to the cross. We respond in truth and in love, helping the other grow in his or her spiritual journey. James 5:16 says, "Therefore, confess your sins to one another and pray for one another, so that you may be healed. The prayer of a righteous person is very powerful in its effect." With Jesus' righteousness covering us and the Holy Spirit dwelling inside us, believers are ambassadors for the kingdom of God. By God's grace, we have the calling and ability to encourage each other toward sanctification which is the day-by-day transformation into the image of Christ. Through private prayer, we engage in God's redemptive work and witness the power of the gospel in another's life.

PRAYING WITH YOUR THOUGHTS

In 1 Thessalonians 5:17, the Apostle Paul commissions believers to "pray constantly." This imperative seems almost impossible to do with the various happenings that take place in a day. It is difficult to assume a posture of prayer when you are in the middle of a board meeting or while you are helping your child with homework. But there is a claim behind Paul's statement that sheds more light on private prayer. With guidance under the Holy Spirit, Paul is teaching us that prayer is not marked just by bowing our heads, closing our eyes, and uttering words aloud. These physical gestures do prepare our hearts, but prayer begins with an inner disposition to commune with God. Our thoughts flow out of the desires of our hearts. So, our thoughts, which run constantly, can be continual prayers to the Lord. Moment by moment, we express gratitude for His salvation and depend on Him for wisdom, strength, or comfort. We can pray this way privately no matter what situation we are in.

Creating a Private Prayer Liturgy

With your discipleship mentor, schedule these times of private prayer.

☐ Spend one hour in private prayer this month. You can go for a walk or sit in a secluded area of your home. Use this time to give your undivided attention to the Lord.

☐ Pray with a friend, family member, or your discipleship mentor this week, confessing to one another your struggles and asking the Lord for help and comfort.

☐ Assess your thought life every day. Choose three specific moments during the day when you can pray to God with your inner thoughts.

"

Corporate prayer is an
opportunity to partner together
in our *worship of God,*
confession of sins, and *requests.*

"

Corporate Prayer

Prayer is a gift given to us by God so that we can communicate with Him. Some may think that prayer is something reserved for a time of solitude as is suggested in Matthew 6:5-6, in contrast to the prayers of the hypocrites. While that is a good discipline of the believer that we explored previously, prayer life is not limited to private prayer. As believers, we are invited to pray with one another in corporate prayer.

Corporate prayer is an opportunity to pray with other believers. If you grew up in the church, you may remember prayers offered aloud in worship services. Perhaps you wondered why the person was offering a prayer aloud, and you were just there to hear it. But corporate prayer is much more than that. Corporate prayer is an opportunity to partner together in our worship of God, confession of sins, and requests. In it, we can be united in the body of Christ, join together in lifting our petitions to the Lord, and learn from the examples of fellow believers.

First, corporate prayer unites us in the body of Christ. We are coming to the Father in one voice to lay our requests before the throne. As believers, we are united to one another by the blood of Christ. He has redeemed us from our sin and joined us together. As Romans 8:17 says, we are "heirs of God and coheirs with Christ." We are fellow heirs together and will spend all of eternity together worshiping God. So as we think in the context of our local bodies, it makes sense that we would be united together. In Paul's letter to the church in Corinth, he pleads, "Now I urge you, brothers and sisters, in the name of our Lord Jesus Christ, that all of you agree in what you say, that there be no divisions among you, and that you be united with the same understanding and the same conviction" (1 Corinthians 1:10). When we pray with one another, divisions should cease because the focus of our prayer should be God Himself. And as we begin to pray together, our desires start to form together and resemble one another. Instead of praying together with our own agendas, we are now coming together as one body, praying that God's will be done, confessing our sin together, and petitioning the Lord to act in mighty ways.

In corporate worship, we pray for one another. In James 5:16, believers are commanded to, "pray for one another." This builds up the body. We pray for one another in our weaknesses—both physically and spiritually. We can join together to pray for spouses and wayward children to come to know the Lord. We can pray for those among us who are suffering, unable to formulate any words. We can lift one another up through sin struggles and be faithful to pray for one another. This is a gift given to us by the Father that we can come to Him on one another's behalf. But praying for one another also gives us the privilege of seeing the Lord answer prayers.

Lastly, praying with other believers affords us the privilege of learning to pray from the example of others in the faith. As we hear the young and old call out to God, we learn from their examples. Hearing their prayers causes us to grow in our own personal prayer lives. The vulnerability shared within the context of corporate prayer is likely to encourage hearers to likewise be vulnerable. As we are growing in our faith, we can also be encouraged by that vulnerability as we see a tangible example of God accepting us as we are and welcoming all of our prayers. As our fellow believers pray, the Spirit can use their words to edify us—causing us to reflect on attributes of God, expose sin in our hearts that we may have otherwise missed, and encourage us to confess our sins and ask for repentance, seeing the fruit of repentance in the lives of the believers around us.

Not all churches have places in their worship service for members to pray. This may be reserved for the pastors or members of the worship team, and your church may not have a prayer service. But do not let that discourage you. In your church services, partner with your pastors or leaders in the prayers being prayed. You can pray in agreement with them as they pray to the Lord. You can also start small and find a few people with whom you can join together and pray.

Read Acts 2:42. To what did the early church devote themselves? Why do you think it was important for them to do that? What lesson could we take away from this Scripture?

_____

_____

_____

_____

_____

_____

_____

Jesus taught His disciples to pray. Who has influenced your prayer life? What things did you take away from his or her prayers that deepened your prayer life? Write a note, thanking that person for faithfully sharing his or her heart in corporate prayer.

_____

_____

_____

_____

_____

_____

_____

Practical step: Where can you participate in corporate prayer? Is it in a Sunday school class or a small group? Ask God to give you the courage to participate in that corporate prayer time.

"

Prayer is *a means of grace* as it allows believers to cultivate intimacy with God.

"

ACTS Model

Prayer is a privilege. It is a means of grace as it allows believers to cultivate intimacy with God. When we pray, we are engaged in sacred communion with Him. Yet, many of us struggle with the discipline of prayer. More often than not, we find ourselves repeating the same things over and over again. Because we feel limited in our language of prayer, we find ourselves reducing it to a Christian formality before meals, during times of need or distress, at formal church gatherings, or before drifting off to sleep. We want to have deep, personal prayer lives, but our minds tend to drift within a few minutes of praying.

Thankfully, prayer is something that we can learn. When we go to Scripture, we see that the disciples asked Jesus to teach them how to pray (Luke 11:1). Jesus responded by offering them the Lord's Prayer. While the Lord's Prayer is a beautiful liturgy for believers to recite, Jesus was offering more than a script for rote recitation. We can deduce this from Scripture because the two accounts of the Lord's prayer recorded in Scripture are not identical (see Matthew 6 and Luke 11). Instead, we see that Jesus was setting forth a principle of prayer. He was offering His disciples (and us!) a framework to guide our prayers. Most of the prayer models that offer a systematic framework for prayer today stem from the principles set forth in the Lord's Prayer.

One simple yet effective model for prayer is the ACTS model. The acrostic stands for adoration, confession, thanksgiving, and supplication. These four categories encompass the various elements of prayer taught in the Lord's Prayer.

ADORATION

We always want to begin our prayers by fixing our eyes on God. When we acknowledge God for who He is, we are placing ourselves in the appropriate posture of humble reverence. Jesus models this in the Lord's prayer by saying, "Our Father in heaven, your name be honored as holy. Your kingdom come" (Matthew 6:9-10). We begin by acknowledging God as our heavenly Father. He is a relational God, and He is for us. He is also above all things, powerful, perfect in all His ways, and worthy of worship. We praise Him for His holiness and pray that others would do the same. Ultimately, that is why we pray: it is all for His glory. When we adore Him for who He is, we are giving Him glory. Starting our prayers with adoration appropriately shapes the rest of our prayers. We set our eyes on eternity first, knowing that everything else will then fall into proper perspective. We want to express our desire for the glory of God to be made known, which is the central goal of the Christian life, before bringing forth our personal requests.

Verses that we can pray to adore God for who He is: Psalm 145, Hebrews 13:8, Psalm 18:30, John 14:6, John 1:1, Hebrews 1:3, Psalm 90:2

CONFESSION

The more we see the glory of God in Scripture, the more we see our utter need for Him. As we begin our prayers, focusing on the truth of God's character, we naturally face the truth that we are not like God. We see our sin more clearly which leads us to confession and repentance. We acknowledge that forgiveness of our sins is required for fellowship with God, and we look to Jesus for forgiveness and relational restoration. While we trust that we have been fully forgiven and redeemed in our union with Christ, we also acknowledge our unredeemed flesh and our failure to love and obey Him perfectly. We specifically acknowledge our sins so that we can turn away from them and turn toward God and the things of God. We also ask the Spirit to help us extend this same forgiveness to those who have wronged us, and we ask Him to help us refrain from falling into future temptation.

Verses to meditate on in our confession: 1 John 1:9, Romans 2:4, 2 Peter 3:9, 1 Corinthians 10:13

THANKSGIVING

Considering the great cost of our redemption as we confess our sins and seek forgiveness, we are naturally led to thanksgiving. As we proclaim the truth of who He is, we are grateful for the fellowship that is offered us in prayer. As we face the truth that we are needy creatures, wholly dependent on Him, we give thanks for His perfect provision, moment by moment.

Verses of thanksgiving: Colossians 4:2, 1 Thessalonians 5:16-18, Psalm 28:7, Psalm 95:1-2, Psalm 34:1-3, Psalm 138:1-2

SUPPLICATION

Supplication is bringing our needs and requests before God. Though God is sovereign, He invites us to bring our very real needs before Him. He desires for us to bring our deep cries of lament and grief to Him in prayer. Jesus is our High Priest who can sympathize with our weaknesses and brokenness (Hebrews 4:15). He knows our frame; our human experience is not beyond Him. He is gentle and lowly (Matthew 11:29), and He invites us to cast all our worries, needs, and desires on Him, trusting in His wisdom to provide what is best for us. We are also invited to petition on behalf of others, approaching the throne of grace with confidence because of our union with Christ. It is right for us to acknowledge that we are needy creatures by God's design. It glorifies God when we look to Him to meet all our needs.

Verses encouraging us to bring our needs to God:
1 Peter 5:7, Philippians 4:6-7, Psalm 121:1-2, Romans 8:32, Hebrews 4:16, James 5:16

The discipline of prayer is something that we can grow in through intentional practice. We learn to pray best by praying ourselves and by listening to others pray. We also believe that the practice of prayer is fueled by knowing who God is as revealed in His Word. No matter our life season, we strive in prayer, endeavoring to make communing with the Lord through prayer a daily reality. We look to the Word of God to guide us, and we believe that our prayers are the means that God uses to spiritually prepare us to receive the things He has for us. We trust in His sovereignty but act on the belief that our prayers matter and move the heart of God.

Practice writing out a prayer using the ACTS model:

Adoration: _____

_____

_____

Confession: _____

_____

_____

_____

Thanksgiving: _____

_____

_____

_____

Supplication: _____

_____

_____

_____

> "
> You will find *great joy*
> in *baring your heart* to the
> God who always hears.
> "

Practicing Prayer

Though it might not be feasible to pray every moment of every day, the encouragement from Scripture points us toward developing a lifestyle of prayer. When you think of the people in your life who are devoted to prayer, you will see a life marked by regular habits of prayer. When prayer is an ingrained part of your daily life, you learn to turn your thoughts and concerns to the Lord over and over throughout the day. You will enjoy His presence and find yourself taking your requests to Him when they come to mind. But like anything in life that we want to become an ingrained habit, a lifestyle of prayer is cultivated by intentional practice.

CONTINUED CONVERSATION

While the concept of regular prayer might feel like a duty or a requirement, the commands to pray should be regarded as an open invitation to conversation with our Father who loves us. If prayer is as simple as talking to Him, and if we are able to do this both aloud and quietly with our thoughts, then we can view unceasing prayer as an ongoing conversation that continues throughout our day. When a concern comes to mind, we can tell the Lord, asking Him to work His good purposes in that situation. When we see a friend who is suffering, we can stop and pray for him or her immediately. When we are afraid or sad, we can cry out to the Lord as soon as those feelings well up within our hearts. When we feel gratitude toward God for something He has done, we can thank Him right away. When temptation entices us to disbelieve God and run after sinful things, we can ask Him to help us resist temptation in the very moment that we feel it. In this ongoing dialogue with God, we are practicing prayer all day long. It will take time, but as we practice turning our thoughts to prayer, we will eventually begin to do so naturally, with less effort.

GROW IN PRAYER BY PRAYING

When we learn an instrument, we practice in order to become proficient. As we play the notes over and over again, the language of music becomes second nature. The same can be true of prayer. We become more faithful in prayer by praying. Though we keep the ongoing conversation with the Lord in our hearts, we will grow in concentration and sincerity when we set aside regular times devoted to nothing but prayer. Jesus regularly slipped away from His disciples and the crowds who followed Him to pray in solitude with God. The intentional nature of Jesus' prayer life encourages us to do the same.

Carving out a regular time of daily prayer is important for spiritual growth. James tells us, "Draw near to God, and He will draw near to you" (James 4:8). Because the Holy Spirit dwells in the heart of every believer, the Lord is always near, but when we intentionally turn our attention to conversation with God, we will be more aware of His presence. Spending regular time in purposeful prayer—where we do nothing else but talk to God—will produce the fruit of peace, joy, and patience in our hearts. Just as our appetites for Scripture increase when we feed them with God's Word, we will desire more frequent and deeper times of prayer when we are regularly giving ourselves to it.

DEVOTED INTERCESSION

Have you ever promised to pray for someone and then promptly forgotten to do so? Paul tells us in Ephesians 6 to pray for other believers, and in 1 Timothy 2, he tells us to pray for all people. In Jesus' high priestly prayer in John 17, He prays for those who will follow Him—including us! The commands and examples of intercession (praying on behalf of others) are many in Scripture. And intercession is important in the life of believers. Praying for others gives us a way to bear the burdens of those who are suffering and a way to pray for unbelievers to come to salvation.

Sometimes intercession can seem a little overwhelming. We forget who we promised to pray for, or we fear that praying for everyone will take up the entire day. A little organization can be helpful—even in your prayer life. Keeping a list for intercession can help us to organize the promises we have made to pray for others and remain faithful to keep them. You might consider dividing requests into days and weeks so that you are interceding for others on a regular basis without feeling overwhelmed. Bearing in mind the privilege and gift of prayer, keeping a list does not have to make prayer a burdensome duty to be checked off each day. A list is simply a tool to practically help you love those you have committed to pray for.

A lifestyle of prayer does not happen overnight. It takes time to cultivate a habit of prayer, but as you carve out time to talk with the Lord each day, keeping up the ongoing conversation, and praying for others, you will enjoy intimacy with God and gratitude for His faithfulness to hear your prayers and to work His good purposes. The practice of prayer might feel like a duty at first, but eventually, you will find great joy in baring your heart to the God who always hears.

Read 1 Thessalonians 5:16-18 and Colossians 4:2-5. What might it look like in your life to be devoted to prayer and to pray constantly?

_____

_____

_____

_____

What are some ways you and your discipleship partner can grow in daily prayer? How might you hold each other accountable?

_____

_____

_____

_____

_____

_____

If you do not have a regular habit of intercession, list some practical ways to grow in that area. What tools (prayer journal, app, calendar, etc.) could you utilize?

_____

_____

_____

_____

_____

Prayer Prompts

Provided is a list to incorporate specific prompts into your prayer life each day. Some of these prompts may not be specific to you (ie. spouse, children, new baby, co-workers, boss, etc.). Use them as an opportunity to pray for someone else or to pray that God would fulfill the desires of your heart for them. Pray through these prompts alone or with someone else. Practice continually including some of these prompts in your prayer life by referencing this page from time to time.

- [ ] Someone you want God to save
- [ ] Sickness you want God to heal
- [ ] Someone you want God to comfort
- [ ] A discipline you want God to strengthen you in
- [ ] A relationship you want God to restore
- [ ] Sin you want God to help you destroy
- [ ] An injustice you desire for God to overcome
- [ ] A means by which you want God to bless someone
- [ ] Spouse
- [ ] Children
- [ ] Parents
- [ ] Siblings
- [ ] Grandparents
- [ ] Neighbors
- [ ] Friends

- [ ] The preservation and faithfulness of the local church
- [ ] Your church family
- [ ] Your pastors and elders
- [ ] Your city, city officials, and community helpers (firefighters, police officers, medical professionals, and teachers)
- [ ] Your state and state officials
- [ ] The President
- [ ] Your job, co-workers, and boss
- [ ] A new believer
- [ ] A non-Christian
- [ ] A missionary
- [ ] A specific ministry
- [ ] A deep love for God's Word
- [ ] Boldness with the Gospel
- [ ] For sanctification and perseverance in the faith
- [ ] For hatred of sin and a delight in obedience

Suggested Next Steps

Provided with the tools to establish a discipleship relationship, our hope is that you would continue meeting and growing in God's Word together after you complete this resource. Since you have already established a relationship, scheduled a time to meet, discussed expectations, and walked through the basics of discipleship, you are well-positioned to continue meeting. We would suggest choosing a book of the Bible to study together and intentionally shaping your time with the key elements we have spent the last four weeks exploring. Though there is flexibility, or freedom, in how you wish to continue your time together, we have provided a suggested outline for how you can structure your meetings.

CHOOSING A BOOK OF THE BIBLE

 Your initial meeting can be spent walking through background information together and discussing the themes and important elements of the book.

 You can decide each week prior to meeting what the reading assignment will be for each time, whether that is a full chapter or a passage of a chapter.

 Prepare for each time by studying the assigned reading on your own (reference: Bible Study Methods on page 73), then use your scheduled meeting time to discuss and apply it together.

Meeting Together

Accountability Questions

- *Choose a few each week to ask (reference: Accountability Questions on page 12). This helps provide a structured way of updating one another on what has transpired in each other's lives since the previous meeting.*

Scripture Memory

- *Choose a verse or passage to memorize each week. We would suggest choosing from the book of the Bible you are studying. Use this time to practice reciting your Scripture memory to one another. It does not have to be perfect but allows you to keep track of your progress.*

Prayer

- *Begin your time in intentional prayer.*

Bible Study Discussion

- *Together, read the assigned chapter or passage.*
- *What did you learn from the assigned reading?*
- *What about the assigned reading was difficult to understand?*
- *Work through Scripture to address any remaining questions together.*
- *Draw out tangible applications (reference: Asking Intentional Application Questions on page 81)*
- *Discuss how you wish to apply these truths to your lives.*

Plan for Next Meeting

- *Reading Assignment*
- *Scripture Memory assignment*
- *How to follow-up with one another throughout the week, whether by sending reminders, checking in about a certain struggle, or simply encouraging one another*
- *Sharing prayer requests*

Prayer

- *Close your time in intentional prayer.*
- *Pray for specific prayer requests.*
- *Pray that God would shape you and change you by the truths uncovered in His Word.*

Additional Resources

Here is a list of recommended resources from The Daily Grace Co. to help structure your continued study of God's Word together.

Be Still Journal

The *Be Still Journal*® is a guided journal for intentional Bible study. This journal can be used on its own or with any Bible study, devotional, or reading plan. The journal includes a section on how to use the journal, as well as sample pages.

The included guided questions and instructions help the reader study any passage of Scripture. The method inside is: Be Still. Abide. Adore. Apply. This method of inductive Bible study helps anyone study the Bible and meet the Lord on the pages of His Word.

Book By Book

Book by Book is a Bible study companion intended to be used when studying a complete book of the Bible. It provides space to fill in background information before you study, key themes, book structure, Scripture to pray during your reading, and reflection for after your study.

Search the Word

God has revealed Himself in His Word, and it is through Scripture that we come to know Him and love Him more. *Search the Word* is a six-week study that equips you with the tools you need to study the Bible for yourself. It walks you through interpretation principles and techniques and includes an abundance of workbook pages allowing you to practice the skills you learn in a hands-on approach. Whether you are brand new to Bible Study or have been studying Scripture for a long time, this study will develop your ability to interpret God's Word faithfully.

In the Word

In the Word is a Biblical exposition journal for in-depth Bible study. The journal guides you through a verse by verse study of a book of the Bible with daily workbook pages and provides prompts to help you understand, interpret, and apply the text, as well as see the connections to Jesus and the gospel.

Scripture Memory Cards

This is a set of 14 Scripture Memory Cards. One side has space to write your Scripture memory verse. The other side has space for you to write the reference and a topic. These are made to be flexible to help you memorize Scripture and carry it with you!

The Bible Handbook

The Bible Handbook is a reference book to help you approach the Bible. This resource includes background and contextual information for each book of the Bible, including literary genre, historical context, purpose, themes, and more. The handbook is complete with summaries of every book of the Bible, maps, and other beautiful graphics and illustrations to enhance your understanding of Scripture.

Bible Studies

The Daily Grace Co. offers a variety of studies to help guide your time in the Word of God. There are studies available on Old Testament and New Testament books, specific topics, and the development of themes throughout Scripture. Each study includes daily Scripture readings, discussion of the passages and topics, and questions to help you reflect on what you have learned.

What is the Gospel?

THANK YOU FOR READING AND ENJOYING THIS STUDY WITH US! WE ARE
ABUNDANTLY GRATEFUL FOR THE WORD OF GOD, THE INSTRUCTION WE
GLEAN FROM IT, AND THE EVER-GROWING UNDERSTANDING ABOUT
GOD'S CHARACTER FROM IT. WE ARE ALSO THANKFUL THAT SCRIPTURE
CONTINUALLY POINTS TO ONE THING IN INNUMERABLE WAYS: THE GOSPEL.

We remember our brokenness when we read about the fall of Adam and Eve in the garden of Eden (Genesis 3), when sin entered into a perfect world and maimed it. We remember the necessity that something innocent must die to pay for our sin when we read about the atoning sacrifices in the Old Testament. We read that we have all sinned and fallen short of the glory of God (Romans 3:23) and that the penalty for our brokenness, the wages of our sin, is death (Romans 6:23). We all are in need of grace and mercy, but most importantly, we all need a Savior.

We consider the goodness of God when we realize that He did not plan to leave us in this dire state. We see His promise to buy us back from the clutches of sin and death in Genesis 3:15. And we see that promise accomplished with Jesus Christ on the cross. Jesus Christ knew no sin yet became sin so that we might become righteous through His sacrifice (2 Corinthians 5:21). Jesus was tempted in every way that we are and lived sinlessly. He was reviled yet still yielded Himself for our sake, that we may have life abundant in Him. Jesus lived the perfect life that we could not live and died the death that we deserved.

The gospel is profound yet simple. There are many mysteries in it that we can never exhaust this side of heaven, but there is still overwhelming weight to its implications in this life. The gospel is the telling of our sinfulness and God's goodness, and this gracious gift compels a response. We are saved by grace through faith, which means

126

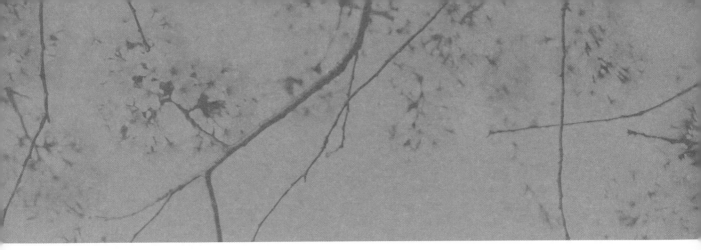

that we rest with faith in the grace that Jesus Christ displayed on the cross (Ephesians 2:8-9). We cannot save ourselves from our brokenness or do any amount of good works to merit God's favor, but we can have faith that what Jesus accomplished in His death, burial, and resurrection was more than enough for our salvation and our eternal delight. When we accept God, we are commanded to die to our self and our sinful desires and live a life worthy of the calling we have received (Ephesians 4:1). The gospel compels us to be sanctified, and in so doing, we are conformed to the likeness of Christ Himself. This is hope. This is redemption. This is the gospel.

SCRIPTURE TO REFERENCE:

GENESIS 3:15
I will put hostility between you and the woman, and between your offspring and her offspring. He will strike your head, and you will strike his heel.

ROMANS 3:23
For all have sinned and fall short of the glory of God.

ROMANS 6:23
For the wages of sin is death, but the gift of God is eternal life in Christ Jesus our Lord.

2 CORINTHIANS 5:21
He made the one who did not know sin to be sin for us, so that in him we might become the righteousness of God.

EPHESIANS 2:8-9
For you are saved by grace through faith, and this is not from yourselves; it is God's gift — not from works, so that no one can boast.

EPHESIANS 4:1
Therefore I, the prisoner in the Lord, urge you to walk worthy of the calling you have received,

*Thank you for studying
God's Word with us!*